Available Titles

ASITPLEASESGOD.COM

Storm Your Brain

Copyright © 2023 by Dr. Y. Bur. All rights reserved.

Visit www.RoarPublishingGroup.com for more information. No part of this publication may be reproduced, stored in a retrieval system, or transmitted in any way by any means, electronic, mechanical, photocopy, recording, or otherwise, without the prior permission of the author except as provided by USA copyright law.

Book design copyright © 2023 by R.O.A.R. International Group. All rights reserved.

R.O.A.R. Publishing Group
581 N. Park Ave. Ste. #725
Apopka, FL 32704
ROAR-58-2316
762-758-2316
www.RoarPublishingGroup.com
DrYBur@gmail.com

Published in the United States of America
ISBN: 978-1-948936-77-4
$22.88

ASITPLEASESGOD.COM

TABLE OF CONTENTS

Introduction 9
BrainStorm 1 11
   Storming Mindset 11
BrainStorm 2 17
   Gratitude Brainiac 17
BrainStorm 3 21
   Overcoming Negative Self-Talk 21
      Reflection 24
      Identifying Triggers 26
BrainStorm 4 37
   Focus On Solutions 37
BrainStorm 5 41
   Embrace Failure 41
BrainStorm 6 47
   Be Realistic 47
      Admit When You Are Wrong 51
BrainStorm 7 53
   Learn Something New 53
BrainStorm 8 59
   Let Go 59
      Expectations 61
BrainStorm 9 65

Cultivating Growth 65

BrainStorm 10 71
Consistency 71

BrainStorm 11 79
Tug-of-War of Beliefs 79

BrainStorm 12 85
Progress, Not Perfection 85

BrainStorm 13 91
Set Boundaries 91

BrainStorm 14 95
Connect With Nature 95

BrainStorm 15 101
Creative Genius 101
Increased Creativity 105

BrainStorm 16 107
Sense Of Humor 107

BrainStorm 17 111
Inner Child 111

BrainStorm 18 115
Spirit to Spirit 115

BrainStorm 19 119
Passionate Purpose 119

BrainStorm 20 125
Peace, Be Still 125

BrainStorm 21 133
Storm Your Brain 133
The Release 137

Thought Conversions 138
Idea Trigger 140
Build-An-Idea Mentality 142
Overcoming Blocks 145
BrainStorm 22 147
Spirit to Business 147
Stay Focused 149
Lift Your Rod 150

INTRODUCTION

Have you ever tried to *Storm Your Brain*? Have you ever had a brain freeze? Are you drawing a blank when pressed to understand your Divine Purpose? Are you confused about life and why you exist? Well, join the crowd; it happens to everyone, even if they pretend they are exempt.

Temporary confusion or failure to perform is normal, causing a brief moment of pain. Meanwhile, *Storming Your Brain* is not a standard practice to alleviate pain, discomfort, or confusion. Why? We are not often taught how to *Storm the Brain* as God intended from the BEGINNING. For this reason, this book lays out the roadmap on how to *Storm Your Brain*, causing it to collaboratively and creatively yield, *As It Pleases Him*.

Storming Your Brain is all about decision-making and problem-solving. According to the MINDSET of *The WHY Blueprint*, we must become experts at making decisions and solving problems. Simply put, we each possess the ability to impact our lives, someone else's life, and the Kingdom of God, no matter how insignificant it may seem. Helping even one person can create a ripple effect of kindness, love, and positivity. Whether volunteering, donating, sharing wisdom, or simply lending a listening ear, every act of kindness makes a difference in the Eye of God. But the kicker is that we need to know what to do, why, and how, without overextending ourselves or having people call us an oxymoron for questioning the questionable.

We cannot live aimlessly with a whatever happens, happens mentality. Nor can we sit back twiddling our thumbs as if we have nothing better to do. According to the Heavenly of Heavens, we all have a reason for being and have something to accomplish. Whether it gets done or not depends on us. Nonetheless, by developing a *Storming Mindset*, we can change the trajectory of our lives by *Overcoming Negative Self-Talk* and becoming a *Gratitude Brainiac*.

Although this *Storming The Brain* approach is a little different, it effectively gets you to *Focus on the Solutions* and *Embrace Failure* like the CHAMPION you already are. The goal is to *Be Realistic* and willing to *Learn Something New* consistently, allowing yourself to *Let Go* of false expectations, preventing you from *Cultivating Growth* pristinely.

In addition, this book's Spiritual Principles and Concepts are designed to help you navigate your Spiritual Path and *Build Your Own Table* with your Gifts, Calling, Talents, and Creativity, *As It Pleases God*, in the Spirit of Excellence. More importantly, if you have not read *The WHY Blueprint* to understand your WHY better, you may miss the relevant information needed to *Storm Your Brain*.

The ultimate purpose is to have the Heavenly of Heavens create an OUTPOURING of information, strategies, concepts, precepts, instructions, secrets, and wisdom, taking you from where you are into Divine Greatness with your Predestined Blueprint. As I reach my hand out to you, let us do this together as ONE, *Spirit to Spirit*!

BRAINSTORM 1

Storming Mindset

We are all familiar with having a Positive Mental Mindset, but what about a *Storming Mindset*? What about thinking on our feet at the drop of a dime? What about devising a plan to save innocent lives? The possibilities are endless if we MASTER the ability to *Storm the Brain*, make it yield, download Divine Instructions, and effectively implement. Do we have the power to do this? Absolutely! This book will share what to do, how to do so, and why we should.

Storming Your Brain is an intense form of brainstorming designed to invoke the Spiritual Elements of your brainial capacity, removing the cobwebs. What if we do not have cobwebs? Unfortunately, we all have them, even if we pretend or think we do not. This is why our brain appears webbed, grooved, and lumpy like waves on water or sound waves. What is the purpose of this? It is connecting with something we do not quite understand yet. By the end of this book, the veiled will be unveiled.

Now the question is, 'What is brainstorming?' Brainstorming is a creative technique to generate ideas, thoughts, concepts, and solutions to problems. It can be a powerful tool for generating new ideas and developing creative solutions to complex issues, with or without God involved in our equational efforts. It can involve one person or a group, sharing thoughts, concepts, and ideas on a particular topic without judgment or criticism. The goal is to produce as many ideas as possible, regardless of how feasible or practical they seem.

On the other hand, *Storming Your Brain* involves God straight out of the gate, Heaven's Gate, to be exact. Why should we involve God? My question would be, 'Why would we NOT involve Him?' He has the Divine Blueprint, knowing our reason for being. If we think we know more than Him, we are sadly mistaken!

In the Beginning, He started with a Divine Plan and will end with one. If we do not up the ante on our problem-solving, decision-making, and negotiating skills, we may forfeit what is hidden within. Why? We must do what is Spiritually Required of us to unleash the creative overflow of Divine Ideas, Thoughts, Wisdom, Creativity, Secrets, and Treasures. Nevertheless, if one desires to remain average, settling for mediocrity, this book is not for them. It is designed to unleash our untapped potential, *As It Pleases God.*

What does negotiation have to do with *Storming the Brain*? If we do not know how to speak to God, leveraging what we know against what He says, we will settle for what we should overcome. Some say we should not question Him or use His word against Him, but I beg to differ! Why would we not have questions? Why would we not use the Word of God? Why would we settle for face value, especially when we have the Spiritual Tools and a *Spirit to Spirit* Relationship to discuss what is what and who is whom?

For example, Abraham negotiates with God over the fate of Sodom and Gomorrah. He presents several scenarios to God to try to save the cities, including asking if He would spare the cities if there were 50, 45, 40, 30, 20, or even 10 righteous people living there. This negotiation shows Abraham's creativity and problem-solving skills as he tries to devise a solution to satisfy himself and God with a win-win.

Building a *Storming Mindset* takes time and effort, taking one step or brick at a time, *Building Your Own Table*. This book will use building blocks or baby steps for those unfamiliar with a blueprinted process. Although the bricks or steps may appear overwhelming at first, they are already written on the tablets of our hearts. Once we awaken ourselves to them, knowing the who, what, when, where, how, and why, it will become natural for us.

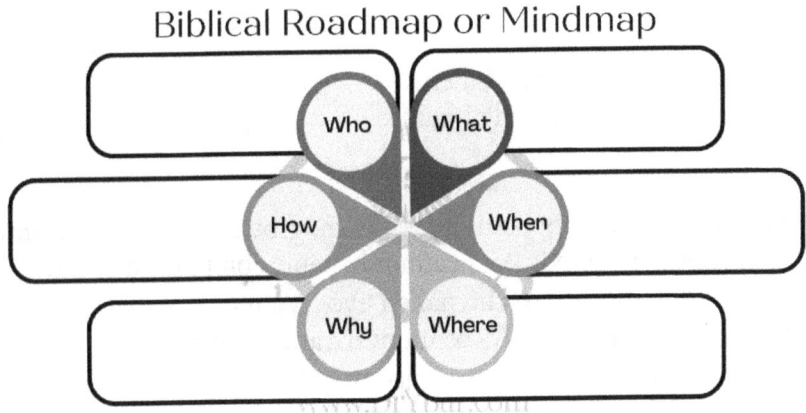

What is the big deal about *Storming the Brain*? Every central character in the Bible did it, and we are not exempt. For example, Noah builds an ark to save his Bloodline...oops, our BLOODLINE. More importantly, in Genesis 6:13-22, God instructs him to build an ark to prepare for the upcoming flood. Noah is given specific dimensions and instructions for the ark, but he must also figure out how to gather the necessary materials and construct the massive vessel. Plus, he had to devise a strategic plan for how to house and care for all of the animals and his family during the flood. Now, the question is, 'Do you think you are any different from Noah?'

The second example is in Genesis 41, when Joseph interprets Pharaoh's dreams and devises a plan to prepare for the upcoming famine. He suggests that Pharaoh appoint someone to oversee the process of storing food during the seven years of plenty so there would be enough to sustain the people during the seven years of famine. Pharaoh and his advisors then discussed and implemented this plan, forging Joseph to the forefront. Here again, the question is, 'Do you think you are any different from Joseph?'

The bottom line is that when God gives us instructions, we must do our part and use what is between our two ears. How?

- ☐ Embrace challenges.
- ☐ Seek feedback.
- ☐ Strive for improvement.
- ☐ Become unafraid of failure.

Everything is an opportunity to learn, grow, and sow back into the Kingdom of God. We cannot become complacent regardless of how life appears to the naked eye. Why? A *Storming Mindset* constantly looks for ways to innovate and create value.

Why is a *Storming Mindset* important? First, a *Storming Mindset* can give you an edge over your competitors in today's fast-paced and competitive world. Secondly, a *Storming Mindset* can help you adapt to changing situations, overcome obstacles, and achieve your goals, boosting your motivation, confidence, and resilience.

How do you develop a Storming Mindset? Use the SWOT chart below to understand your Strengths, Weaknesses, Opportunities, and Threats.

Date: _____   Day: _____

SWOT Analysis

Strengths

_____
_____
_____
_____
_____

Weaknesses

_____
_____
_____
_____
_____

Opportunities

_____
_____
_____
_____
_____

Threats

_____
_____
_____
_____
_____

A *Storming Mindset* can help you achieve your personal, professional, and Spiritual goals. It can also help you enjoy your Spiritual Journey and the learning that comes with it.

Storming Your Brain is a valuable tool, especially when the Cycles and Vicissitudes of Life become challenging feats, when solving complex problems, or when becoming a *Gratitude Brainiac*. However, this storming level is not something you are born with. Still, it can be developed with practice and persistence. Start today and unleash your Divine Potential!

BRAINSTORM 2
Gratitude Brainiac

How do you begin your day? Are you dreading waking up in the morning? Do you have a plan for your day? Do you dictate your day, or does it dictate you? By becoming a *Gratitude Brainiac*, we can change the trajectory of our lives with character traits that move the Heart of God.

Why should we move the Heart of God? Having the Mind of God is not easy, nor is it safe to tap into the Mind of God without MANAGING and MASTERING ours first. No judgment is intended, but if negativity, emotionalism, disobedience, and lies flow through our veins, it is best not to get into God's Headspace until we work on ourselves, *As It Pleases Him*. Blasphemy, right? Wrong.

With the Mind of Christ, we must heed Divine Instructions to download from the Heavenly of Heavens. Is this Biblical? Absolutely! *"For 'who has known the mind of the LORD that he may instruct Him?' But we have the mind of Christ."* 1 Corinthians 2:16. Here is why: *"But we speak the wisdom of God in a mystery, the hidden wisdom which God ordained before the ages for our glory, which none of the rulers of this age knew; for had they known, they would not have crucified the Lord of glory."* 1 Corinthians 2:7-8.

Why should we not get into God's Headspace as Believers? Whether we are Believers or not, trying to outsmart Him with our antics is a quick way to turn against ourselves without realizing it, especially if we do not use the Fruits of the Spirit, behave Christlike, or do not utilize the Holy Trinity as we should. He says, *"For My thoughts are not your thoughts, Nor are your ways My ways, says the Lord. For as the heavens are higher than the earth, So are My ways higher than your ways, And My thoughts than your thoughts."* Isaiah 55:8-9. For this reason, getting into the Heart is much easier and rewarding.

Starting each day with gratitude helps us to appreciate the good things in our lives and focus on the positive aspects of our day. Why? It has a Spiritual Seal attached: *"But as it is written: 'Eye has not seen, nor ear heard, Nor have entered into the heart of man The things which God has prepared for those who love Him.'"* 1 Corinthians 2:9. Simply put, gratefulness opens closed doors, and ungratefulness closes open doors.

With this same analogy, the brain is designed to yield when we are grateful for its use. Here again, gratefulness opens a closed brainiac mind, and ungratefulness closes it. With this being said, if one wants to be in the know with our Heavenly Father, here is what we must know: *"But God has revealed them to us through His Spirit. For the Spirit searches all things, yes, the deep things of God. For what man knows the things of a man except the spirit of the man which is in him? Even so no one knows the things of God except the Spirit of God. Now we have received, not the spirit of the world, but the Spirit who is from God, that we might know the things that have been freely given to us by God."* 1 Corinthians 2:10-12.

How can we make this make sense? The bottom line is that for all things Spiritual, we need DISCERNMENT. *"But the natural man does not receive the things of the Spirit of God, for they are foolishness to him; nor can he know them, because they are spiritually discerned."* 1 Corinthians 2:14. Our brainial capacity is hidden within our discerning faculties, which depend upon our conscience and senses. Therefore, we do not want them to become desensitized. Why? Our brainiac capacity is our money-making power; one would never want to lose one's conscience in this area. What does this mean? The Bible says, *"What profit is it to a man if he gains the whole world, and loses his own soul?"* Matthew 16:26.

My question is, 'How many times have you thanked your money?' I bet you have lost count of how many times you have extended gratitude toward your cash flow. Here is another question: 'How many times have you thanked your brain?' Yet, it produces without fail, and we have the nerves to forget to say, 'Thank you.' For this reason, it does the bare minimum, causing us to use less than 10% of its capacity. What about the other 90%? Once again, it is primarily Spiritual!

We are Spiritual Beings having a human experience; by omitting our Spiritual Side, *As It Pleases God*, we lose Divine Access to maximize our brainial capacity. How so? We are created in the Image of God; if we deny our Kingdom Status, we cannot get Divine Access just because we want it. We must Spiritually Till our own ground.

With all due respect, in the Realm of the Spirit, we are walking around Spiritually Brain-Dead in the Eye of God. Really? Yes, really! We have to do better! I am not here to point the finger...I was in the same shoes until I was forced to use other areas of my brain to SURVIVE. So, I know the difference, and it is my reasonable service to share what I know to get those who are WILLING in the Divine Know.

Knowing what I now know, I will lay out a roadmap on how to *Storm The Brain*, but it is left up to us to walk it out. What if we choose not to? We will be left behind, wallowing when we can ride the waves or walk on water.

Can we really walk on water? Let me counteract this question with another: 'Can we really drown?' If one does not know how to swim, they could drown. Then again, if they lack faith in their ability to swim, they still can drown. Here is what we must know: *"And immediately Jesus stretched out His hand and caught him, and said to him, 'O you of little faith, why did you doubt?'"* Matthew 14:31. This story is about Peter walking on water towards Jesus, but then becoming afraid, doubtful, and starting to sink. Jesus reaches out and saves him, while rebuking him for his lack of faith. It reminds us to trust and focus on God even in complex, challenging, or dark situations.

On the other hand, if one has the right Spiritual Tools, *As It Pleases God*, nothing is impossible. Why? God will move Heaven and Earth to save us, especially if we are in Purpose on purpose according to our Predestined Blueprint. Here is a Gratitude Reflection Chart to assist:

GRATITUDE REFLECTION

WHAT ARE YOU GRATEFUL FOR TODAY?	WHAT DO YOU LOVE ABOUT YOURSELF?	WHAT ARE YOU EXCITED ABOUT?

The *Gratitude Brainiac Chart* can help improve our overall outlook and increase our well-being, *As It Pleases God*. By taking a few moments each morning to reflect on what we are thankful for, we can set a positive tone for the day ahead, approaching challenges with a more optimistic mindset while *Overcoming Negative Self-Talk*.

BRAINSTORM 3
Overcoming Negative Self-Talk

What are you saying about you? Are you your best cheerleader or worst dictator? Is your mental chatter driving you insane? Is your mouth getting you in more trouble than you care to imagine? Are you putting your mouth on others to destroy them? Is false propaganda ruling your life? Do you know the difference between positive and negative words, thoughts, behaviors, or demeanor? Most know the difference, and some do not; therefore, in this chapter, we leave no man behind to question the gateway of negativity or positivity.

The biggest hurdle we will face is dealing with negativity. It is like a plague, affecting everything we come in contact with. Unfortunately, there is no way around it; therefore, we must learn how to go through it, *As It Pleases God*. Here is what we must do, but not limited to such:

1. We must identify the source.
2. We must challenge it.
3. We must reinforce it with positivity.

Can this really help us? Absolutely. Once we identify the source, we can challenge it with the Word of God, positive affirmations, or the opposite of whatever. The key is to do it without allowing negativity to fester, causing us to wax cold. Really? Yes, really! Please allow me to Spiritually Align: "*And because iniquity shall abound, the love of many shall wax cold. But he that shall endure unto the end, the same shall be saved.*" Matthew 24:12-13. For this reason, we must deflect negativity as much as possible. Here is a Negativity Deflection Chart:

Why is negativity so harmful to the human psyche? It is a distraction for deceptive measures of manipulation, bullying, and whitewashing. If we do nothing about it, innocent people are affected massively. Listen, the nature of the beast is not looking for captives; they are designed to take out the weak, naive, and abandoned. Unfortunately, this is similar to the animalistic nature of the wild, spotting the weak and taking them out to feed their BLOODLINE.

We must change the way we speak to ourselves and others. Why? The moment we open our mouths, the heart's content spills out. If not on the positive side of the spectrum, it can cause us to doubt ourselves, feel anxious, fearful, or depressed, and even hold us back from achieving our goals. To replace negative self-talk, we can start by identifying the negative thoughts, words, and beliefs about ourselves and replacing them with positive ones. The negative conversion chart to *Storm Your Brain* is below.

STORM YOUR BRAIN
Negative Conversions

NEGATIVE		POSITIVE
	⟶	
	⟶	
	⟶	
	⟶	
	⟶	
	⟶	
	⟶	
	⟶	
	⟶	
	⟶	
	⟶	
	⟶	
	⟶	
	⟶	
	⟶	
	⟶	
	⟶	
	⟶	
	⟶	
	⟶	
	⟶	

Continue this process until your brain autocorrects negativity. If you choose not to document, measuring your growth and reflecting will become problematic. Why? You will tend to forget. Yes, forget about what you did or said. Then again, it may be forgetting what must be said or done. Who knows, besides the Spiritual Mirror reflecting our blind reflectors. What does this mean? We become slightly blinded by our triggers, like a deer blinded by a car's headlights. Really? Yes, really!

We can get ourselves in deep trouble if we do not know our triggers. Why? It means the psyche is in complete control, our conscience has gone silent, and we have become desensitized Mentally, Physically, or Emotionally. Is this humanly possible? Absolutely! We will naturally adapt to anything or anyone with time; however, adapting to drama, trauma, chaos, and confusion is not normal, especially in the Eye of God. So, let us go deeper...

Reflection

When we think about reflecting, we often overlook the human psyche. Why? We are not trained to approach ourselves and life from the inside out. Unfortunately, we are taught to approach from the outside in, which creates a disservice to the Kingdom of God.

Our heart posture is what God is looking for, and if we have not unbundled the Fruits of the Spirit, knowing nothing about them, it is fair to say we have quirks that are displeasing to Him. What does this mean? When we are pleasing ourselves first, it is apparent we are not *Pleasing God*.

When reflecting, *As It Pleases God*, we must become a work-in-progress instead of an already self-made protege. Why? When approaching Him with pompousness, it is a possibility that He may ghost us or go silent on us. Would He really do this to us? Absolutely! When we are disobedient, dull, stiff-necked, rebellious, debaucherous, conniving, or have an ungoverned tongue, He will remain silent as we dig our own pits.

Why would God leave us to dig our own pits? Unfortunately, He did not create us as robots; we were created to have free will. All this means is that we can make our own choices; therefore, He will leave us to our own devices until we call out to Him and pull out our Spiritual Mirror to reflect. For example, Psalm 28:1 says, "*To You I will cry, O Lord my Rock: Do not be silent to me, Lest, if You are silent to me, I become like those who go down to the pit.*' Here is another one, "*Hear my prayer, O LORD, And give ear to my cry; Do not be silent at my tears; For I am a stranger with You, A sojourner, as all my fathers were. Remove Your gaze from me, that I may regain strength, Before I go away and am no more.*" Psalm 39:12-13.

To begin reflecting, *As It Pleases God*, find a quiet and comfortable space to focus without distractions. Take a few deep breaths and clear your mind of clutter or stress. Then, determine what you are laying on the Altar of God. Before completing the Reflection Chart below, repeat this: "*I will instruct you and teach you in the way you should go; I will guide you with My eye.*" Psalm 32:8. Then document, *Spirit to Spirit*.

Storm Your Brain Reflection Chart

What I Learned	Questions I Have	Next Steps
✓	?	》
✓	?	》
	?	》
✓	?	》
✓	?	》

How do we align growth with reflection? By identifying limiting beliefs or negative self-talk, we can shift our mindset towards a more positive and growth-oriented perspective. On the other hand, if we do not know what to do, we will begin to fill in the blanks with folly, contradicting the Will of God or our Divine Blueprint.

For the record, not all mindsets are conducive to growth. Some mindsets are fixed, believing their abilities and potential are predetermined and unchangeable. Meanwhile, in the Kingdom, we must remain flexible, teachable, understandable, relatable, tolerable, and approachable. Why? In the Eye of God, when overcoming a negative mindset with Divine Greatness, we must become Kingdomly Usable to feed His sheep in the Spirit of Excellence.

Why must we operate in the Spirit of Excellence? A Mind of Greatness possesses exceptional intelligence, creativity, and leadership skills. So, we cannot approach God with shabbiness similar to the Spirit of Cain, presenting Him with anything as if He should accept it, as-is. According to the Heavenly of Heavens, He will reject it and us for disrespecting Him. Why? He has given us the ability to achieve great things through a developmental process; the least we can do is use it!

When we are focused, determined, and driven to succeed, we can crush the limits and triggers holding us back from our Divine Blueprinted Purpose.

Identifying Triggers

No one is exempt from triggers; we all have them. But we do not often know how to deal with or contain them to enhance our self-awareness, self-confidence, self-regulation, and self-control, *As It Pleases God*.

What is the purpose of understanding our triggers? It can help clarify our visions, values, standards, and purpose, giving new insights, perspectives, and solutions according to Kingdom Standards and not our own. In addition, knowing our triggers can help us better understand our reactions, traumas, and behaviors.

By identifying our triggers, we can learn to recognize when we are being triggered and develop strategies to manage our responses accordingly. Above all, properly managing our triggers can help us communicate more effectively with God, ourselves, and others, avoiding unnecessary distress, conflict, or charactorial sabotage. James 1:19-20 says, "*So then, my beloved brethren, let every man be swift to hear, slow to speak, slow to wrath; for the wrath of man does not produce the righteousness of God.*"

How can we break a negative pattern or habit? Breaking a negative pattern or habit can be challenging, but it is possible with effort and dedication. It starts with identifying the pattern or habit and understanding the triggers leading to it. When *Storming Your Brain*, there are three types of triggers we will deal with:

1. Bodily Triggers.
2. Anger Triggers.
3. Depression Triggers.

Knowing about our triggers is not always easy or comfortable, but it is essential for self-awareness and psyche regulation. Proverbs 29:11 says, "*A fool vents all his feelings, But a wise man holds them back.*" According to the Heavenly of Heavens, impulsive or unwise behavior is a big no-no in the Eye of God. So, let us dig deeper to understand Kingdom Expectations better.

Bodily Triggers

Do you know what triggers you? Do you know what does not trigger you? Have you paid attention to your triggers? Do you know what triggers are?

Bodily triggers are physical sensations responding to uncontrolled emotions, thoughts, beliefs, traumas, or conditioning. They can be unpleasant, uncomfortable, or even painful, interfering with our daily functioning and our Spiritual Relationship with God. Triggers, as such, are often linked to challenging experiences, stress, anxiety, or fear, and can also occur for other reasons. Once you have identified these triggers, you can work on developing new habits and patterns. Here are a few of the most common bodily triggers, but not limited to such:

- ☐ Loud noises.
- ☐ Bright lights.
- ☐ Strong smells.
- ☐ Certain tastes.
- ☐ Physical touch.
- ☐ Crowded spaces.
- ☐ Social situations.
- ☐ Feeling rushed or overwhelmed.
- ☐ Seeing certain objects.
- ☐ Hearing specific words or phrases.
- ☐ Memories of traumatic events.
- ☐ Feeling hot or cold.
- ☐ Hunger or thirst.
- ☐ Stressful situations.
- ☐ Sleeping problems.
- ☐ Hormonal changes.
- ☐ Certain medications.
- ☐ Allergies.
- ☐ Physical pain.
- ☐ Emotional distress.

What if we do not know our triggers? If you do not know your triggers, it is okay. It may take some time and self-reflection to identify them. One helpful approach is to keep a journal, noting when you engage in a negative pattern, responses, or habits. Also document when experiencing tightness in the chest, nausea, sweating, trembling, fragmented thoughts, brain fogs, rapid heartbeats, or any negative feelings.

Anger Triggers

Do you see red when you become angry? Do you experience mental sparks or flames when you become enraged? Do you sweat or become fuming hot when infuriated? Then again, do you outright lose it? Do you destroy everything and everyone in your path when you are triggered?

Anger is a normal emotion we experience from time to time. Why? It is a survival mechanism to preserve, save, or elevate our lives. Ephesians 4:26 says, *"Be angry, and do not sin: do not let the sun go down on your wrath."* However, some people may struggle to manage and express their anger in healthy and constructive ways. This type of anger is not typical if it provokes Mental, Physical, Emotional, and Spiritual lapses leading to uncontrollable reactions or outbursts, causing us to get a side-eye from God Almighty. When becoming angry in such a manner, here is what Ecclesiastes 7:9 says, *"Do not hasten in your spirit to be angry, For anger rests in the bosom of fools."*

We have work to do if our anger is destroying, degrading, or unraveling ourselves or others. Why? God looks for our heart posture, and if it is keeled with outbursts similar to Moses striking the rock when he was supposed to speak to it, in Numbers 20:7-12, it is outright disobedience in the Eye of God. Why? When He gives specific instructions, it is best to obey than to allow our anger to get the best of us.

Anger triggers will vary from person to person, depending on their personality, thoughts, conditioning, traumas, temperament, coping skills, beliefs, understanding, and life experiences. Some may have more anger triggers than others, but in the Eye of God, a trigger is a trigger.

For example, some people may have difficulty identifying or expressing their emotions, feelings, thoughts, or beliefs. Then again, some may have unresolved emotional issues from the past, making them more prone to anger. Others may have negative or distorted thinking patterns fueling their anger, such as blaming others, jumping to conclusions, overgeneralizing, taking things personally, or exhibiting the crabs in the bucket mentality.

Unfortunately, some are conditioned to use anger to cope with stress, communicate their needs, get attention from others, or manipulate others. The bottom line is that understanding our anger triggers helps us manage our anger more effectively and prevent it from escalating into harmful behaviors.

We also must consider those who have rigid or unrealistic beliefs that clash with reality or with other people's perspectives, such as:

- ☐ I am always right and never wrong.
- ☐ I never make mistakes.
- ☐ I can say what I want.
- ☐ I can do whatever I want.
- ☐ People should always do what I want them to do.
- ☐ People should always follow me, doing what I do.
- ☐ If I cannot manipulate them, they are against me.

According to the Heavenly of Heavens, we all have free will, but it does not justify or condone bullying or manipulation, period. Why? If God did not make us robots, then we should not make His sheep robotically traumatized by our unresolved or unregulated triggers.

According to *The WHY Blueprint*, we can become defeated when we think we do not have triggers. Why? *The WHY Blueprint* says, 'What Hurts Us is What Heals Us.' Therefore, we all have something to work on or work at, and if we are not using the Fruits of the Spirit or behaving Christlike, our underlying triggers will wreak havoc on us and our Bloodline. Proverbs 15:1 says, "*A soft answer turns away wrath, But a harsh word stirs up anger.*" So, when dealing with anger, here are the most common triggers:

- ☐ When feeling disrespected or left out.
- ☐ Being treated unfairly or unjustly.
- ☐ When feeling threatened or attacked.
- ☐ Not being listened to or heard.

- ☐ When feeling powerless or helpless.
- ☐ Being interrupted or ignored.
- ☐ When you feel like your boundaries are being violated.
- ☐ When feeling like someone is not taking responsibility for their actions.
- ☐ When being questioned or attacked.
- ☐ You feel like you are not appreciated or valued.
- ☐ Dishonesty or deceitfulness.
- ☐ Being manipulated or controlled.
- ☐ When someone is being condescending or patronizing.
- ☐ When someone is being hypocritical.
- ☐ When someone is being insensitive or uncaring.
- ☐ When someone is being rude.
- ☐ When someone is being dismissive or sarcastic.
- ☐ When someone is being aggressive or hostile.
- ☐ When someone is being judgmental or critical.
- ☐ When someone is being selfish or self-centered.
- ☐ When someone is intentionally belittling you.
- ☐ When someone is yelling or cussing at you.
- ☐ When someone takes your kindness for a weakness.
- ☐ When someone unjustifiably throws you under the bus.

Over time, you may notice specific patterns or situations that trigger negative behaviors; make sure you document them. Why? To *Storm Your Brain* properly, you must become AWARE of them to ensure the enemy does not use your overlooked triggers as a weakness or loophole to place depressive yokes, soul ties, or leverage bondage.

Depression Triggers

Are you depressed? Are you fighting off depression? Do you place your depression on others to project or deflect? Do you make the lives of others miserable or better? Do you feel defeated, wearing all types of masks to cover it up?

In certain cultures, they look at depression as some form of taboo, but it is not. We all possess this charactorial trait or hormonal imbalance that causes us to ponder, rethink, reevaluate, or redo, similar to an online program rebuffering or a car about to run out of gas, letting us know it is time to refuel. Nevertheless, the difference is in how long we remain in this condition. It can last a few seconds, hours, days, months, years, or a lifetime. Some depression falls under a mental health condition, and most of it does not. Why not? Most of it is due to the lack of self-control, understanding, know-how, and Spirituality.

According to the Bible, King David was transparent about his depressive triggers. For this reason, if we do not know or understand this trigger, we can become an enemy to ourselves, allowing negative triggers to consume us Mentally, Physically, Emotionally, Spiritually, or Financially.

Depression triggers are derived from uncontrolled emotions, thoughts, beliefs, traumas, or conditioning. Unfortunately, there are times when our triggers can become overwhelming, intense, or difficult to manage, especially when we keep feeding them negatively. How do we know if we are susceptible to negative triggers? Here are a few reasons, but not limited to such:

- We have negative, irrational, or distorted thinking, affecting our mood and behavior.
- We have uncontrolled negative beliefs, thoughts, or words.
- We make irrational assumptions without having the facts or asking questions.
- Our expectations are unrealistic, rigid, biased, or self-defeating.
- We feel hopeless, helpless, worthless, or guilty.
- We self-sabotage everything with everyone.
- We have rotten fruits all over the place without realizing they are rotten.

- ☐ We are angry, anxious, or grieving.
- ☐ We are ruminating over the same mistakes, failures, or regrets.
- ☐ We feel unworthy, inadequate, or undesirable.
- ☐ We are perfectionists.
- ☐ We are suffering from prolonged neglect or abandonment.

Susceptibility does not need to become our vulnerability. Really? Yes, really! The Holy Spirit, the Word of God, the Fruits of the Spirit, and behaving Christlike are our lifeline. Isaiah 41:10 says, *"Fear not, for I am with you; Be not dismayed, for I am your God. I will strengthen you, Yes, I will help you, I will uphold you with My righteous right hand."*

When *Storming The Brain*, we must pinpoint our triggers to strengthen our vulnerable areas; we cannot bury them and think they will disappear. Why? They are seeds, roots, fruits, or trees; therefore, they must be uprooted, regrafted, or pruned, *As It Pleases God*. Matthew 11:28-30 says, *"Come to Me, all you who labor and are heavy laden, and I will give you rest. Take My yoke upon you and learn from Me, for I am gentle and lowly in heart, and you will find rest for your souls. For My yoke is easy and My burden is light."* Remember, *Depression Triggers* will vary from person to person; however, we must master the triggers to effectively deal with the seed, root, fruit, or cause of the condition. Here are a few of the most common depression triggers, but not limited to such:

- ☐ Stressful life events.
- ☐ Loss of a loved one.
- ☐ A divorce.
- ☐ Financial difficulties.
- ☐ Chronic illness or physical pain.
- ☐ Genetics and family history of depression.
- ☐ Traumatic experiences, like abuse or neglect.
- ☐ Social isolation or loneliness.

- ☐ Alcohol or drug use.
- ☐ Hormonal changes due to menopause.
- ☐ Pregnancy.
- ☐ Lack of exercise or physical activity.
- ☐ Poor nutrition and unhealthy eating habits.
- ☐ Sleep disturbances or insomnia.
- ☐ Chronic stress or burnout.
- ☐ Work-related stress or job dissatisfaction.
- ☐ Certain medications, such as those used to treat high blood pressure or cholesterol.
- ☐ Seasonal changes and lack of sunlight.
- ☐ Lack of social support or a strong social network.
- ☐ Negative thought patterns and self-talk.
- ☐ Anxiety or panic disorders.
- ☐ Feelings of guilt, shame, or worthlessness.
- ☐ Past trauma or abuse.
- ☐ Existing mental health conditions.

You can also try talking with a trusted friend or professional who can provide an outside perspective and help you identify potential triggers. In *Storming Your Brain*, the goal is to understand the underlying seed, root, fruit, or causes of the behavior so that you can work on changing it and focus on the solution of whatever with whomever. Here is a chart to assist in tracking your triggers.

STORM YOUR BRAIN
TRIGGER TRACKER

DATE _____

| Mon | Tue | Wed | Thu | Fri | Sat | Sun |

1
WHY? _____
TRIGGER _____
_____
_____

2
WHY? _____
TRIGGER _____
_____
_____

3
WHY? _____
TRIGGER _____
_____
_____

4
WHY? _____
TRIGGER _____
_____
_____

5
WHY? _____
TRIGGER _____
_____
_____

6
WHY? _____
TRIGGER _____
_____
_____

STORM YOUR BRAIN
Trigger List

- [ ] What Triggers Me?
- [ ] What Triggers Me?
- [ ] What Triggers Me?
- [ ] What Triggers Me?
- [ ] What Triggers Me?
- [ ] What Triggers Me?
- [ ] What Triggers Me?
- [ ] What Triggers Me?
- [ ] What Triggers Me?
- [ ] What Triggers Me?
- [ ] What Triggers Me?
- [ ] What Triggers Me?
- [ ] What Triggers Me?
- [ ] What Triggers Me?
- [ ] What Triggers Me?
- [ ] What Triggers Me?
- [ ] What Triggers Me?

BRAINSTORM 4
Focus On Solutions

How are your solution or resolution skills? Do you wallow over problems? Are you able to create a win-win out of a not-so-great situation? Can you reverse engineer a negative thought, feeling, or desire? When *Storming Your Brain*, focusing on positive, productive, and fruitful aspects of a situation, circumstance, event, or person is imperative, primarily when solving, addressing, or creating solutions. Why? Divine Wisdom is hidden in everything; therefore, our approach will determine if whatever we need will yield to us.

Storming The Brain aims to get the information we need to flow to, through, and around us; thus, we must condition our mindset to receive. Why is this so important? Simply put, like attracts like. If we focus on problems, we will inadvertently attract problematic energy. On the other hand, if we are solution-oriented, we will graft in solution-oriented energy.

A solution-oriented mindset does not mean problems do not find their way into our camp; it means that if the problem comes, it must ATTACH the solution. If one does not know this Spiritual Fact, they cannot put a demand on it. What does this mean? If we are unaware of a Spiritual Law, we cannot enforce it. Nor can we hold anyone in contempt for violating it or judge others for knowing what we failed to learn. How do we make this make sense? For example, if someone hurts our feelings, and we take it to God in prayer, asking for retribution without understanding the details, we can pray amiss. For example, here are a few things to know, but not limited to such:

- ☐ What feelings did they hurt?
- ☐ Why were we hurt?
- ☐ What triggered the hurt?
- ☐ How did it create discomfort?
- ☐ Where in the Bible does this align with the justification?
- ☐ What was our role in the situation?
- ☐ How did we apply the Fruits of the Spirit to this situation?
- ☐ Did we behave Christlike amid the encounter?

What is up with all the questions? To become solution-oriented, we must force our brainiac minds to think quickly, gathering relevant information. Why? When taking our qualms to God, we often take them amissly, emotionally, and selfishly. Here is the deal: there are three sides to every story.

- ☐ Our side.
- ☐ Their side.
- ☐ The TRUTH.

When *Storming The Brain*, we must do our best to gather all the relevant information by asking fact-finding questions without assuming. Why? We DO NOT think alike! For example, when people try to tell my story or reverberate what I am thinking, they get it all wrong because they never asked me. I think, behave, speak, and operate differently than most; therefore, no one can put their perception or opinion about me in writing or their words in my mouth as fact. More importantly, I do not try to correct them, as long as I know the truth, *As It Pleases God*, there is no need to correct foolery.

When we are ten toes deep in the Kingdom, *As It Pleases God*, we must glean wisdom, knowledge, and understanding by asking fact-finding questions while DOCUMENTING it accordingly to get solutions.

Why are questions so important? Every solution has a seed, root, tree, and fruit, creating a Symbolic Action Plan. When we focus on the problem, we often get bogged down with negative emotions, thoughts, and outcomes. Thus, a Symbolic Action Plan creates a questionable flow from point A to point B, ensuring we can create a mind map, roadmap, or whatever we need to document our progress or solution. Here is an example:

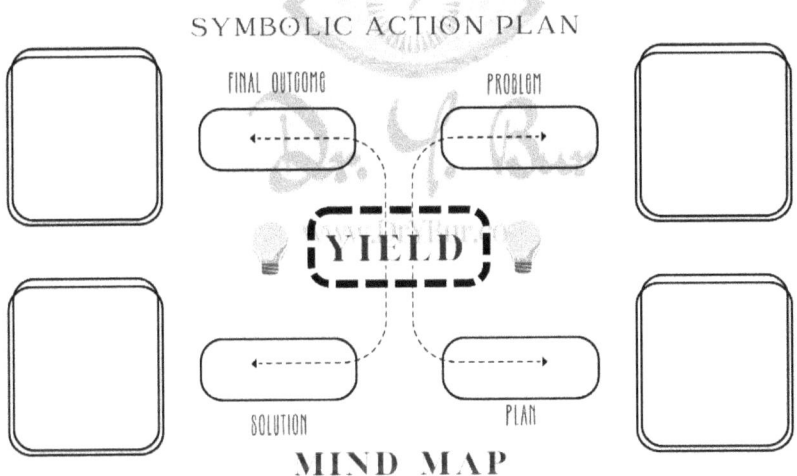

By focusing on the solution, we shift our attention to what we can do to improve things or create a win-win. This approach helps us feel empowered, but it also helps us identify the steps we can take to move forward or the bricks needed to build.

BRAINSTORM 5
Embrace Failure

Do you despise failing? Do you feel it is a blow to your ego to fail? Do you learn from your failures? Are you ready to flourish? Are you ready to embrace your Divine Birthright?

Most think failure is doom, but it is not. Let me repeat: IT IS NOT! Unbeknown to most, what fails you is what flourishes you, but you must know this. If not, one may become dry, dull, and chaff, blown away by the wind of mediocrity.

No one is exempt from this Spiritual Principle of FLOURISHING unless they exempt themselves by not knowing, understanding, or enforcing it, *As It Pleases God.* How can we exempt ourselves? When we become bound by our Spiritual Woes, exemption can occur. Is this Biblical? I would have it no other way. *"Woe to those who call evil good, and good evil; Who put darkness for light, and light for darkness; Who put bitter for sweet, and sweet for bitter! Woe to those who are wise in their own eyes, And prudent in their own sight! Woe to men mighty at drinking wine, Woe to men valiant for mixing intoxicating drink, Who justify the wicked for a bribe, And take away justice from the righteous man! Therefore, as the fire devours the stubble, And the flame consumes the chaff, So their root will be as rottenness, And their* blossom will ascend like dust; Because they have rejected the law of the LORD of hosts, And despised the word of the Holy One of Israel." Isaiah 5:20-24.

When *Storming The Brain*, failure is an opportunity filled with information, understanding, knowledge, and wisdom for us to Spiritually Flourish. Then again, it may be our Spiritual Training Ground or Classroom that God has designed to smooth out our rough edges for personal and professional growth. Here is the Spiritual Seal: *"Blessed is the man who walks not in the counsel of the ungodly, nor stands in the path of sinners, nor sits in the seat of the scornful; but his delight is in the law of the Lord, and in His law he meditates day and night. He shall be like a tree planted by the rivers of water, that brings forth its fruit in its season, whose leaf also shall not wither; and whatever he does shall prosper."* Psalm 1:1-3.

Instead of dwelling on our mistakes and shortcomings, we can view them as learning experiences, stepping stones, and training. Failure allows us to reflect on what went wrong, understand our weaknesses, and develop a plan to improve. By embracing failure, we can become more resilient, better problem-solvers or resolvers, and more determined to achieve our goals. So do not be afraid to fail; use it as an opportunity to grow and succeed while grabbing the hidden nuggets of wisdom.

The orchestration behind failure is trusting God, even when we cannot trace him. Why? It builds faith. Without faith, we cannot unveil our Predestined Blueprint because it takes blind obedience to break the Spiritual Seal on our Blueprinted Purpose. Here is what Jeremiah 17:7-8 says, *"Blessed is the man who trusts in the Lord, and whose hope is the Lord. For he shall be like a tree planted by the waters, which spreads out its roots by the river, and will not fear when heat comes; but its leaf will be green, and will not be anxious in the year of drought, nor will cease from yielding fruit."*

The Spiritual Yield associated with *Storming The Brain* is unlike any other harvest known to man. Why? When rooted in God's Word and His Divine Promises, *As It Pleases Him*, flourishing comes with the territory. What if we are not flourishing? We are still in training and testing mode. If this is the case, just make sure you are:

- ☐ Placing the Holy Trinity first.
- ☐ Using all of the Fruits of the Spirit.
- ☐ Behaving Christlike.
- ☐ Repenting.
- ☐ Forgiving.
- ☐ Exhibiting a Positive Mental Mindset.
- ☐ Spiritually Aligning with the Word of God.
- ☐ Sharing with others.
- ☐ Spiritually Tilling your own ground.
- ☐ Guarding the gateway of your mouth.
- ☐ Willing to become a work-in-progress.
- ☐ Documenting.

Above all, we must ensure we are reverse-engineering our failures. How so? By creating a win-win situation through change, growth, sharing, and turning our failures into a flourishing expectation, *As It Pleases God*. Romans 8:28 says, "*And we know that all things work together for good to those who love God, to those who are the called according to His purpose.*" Even difficult or painful experiences can be used for our ultimate good and God's glory; however, we may have to search for them. Why is searching necessary? The potential for growth, transformation, and flourishing exists amid challenging situations.

Life is not about denying or ignoring our challenges, but instead focusing on the solutions and embracing the benefits. In *Storming The Brain*, we are also moving from a scarcity mindset, where we see everything as a competition, struggle, or a game, to an abundance mindset, where we see everything as an opportunity, a lesson, and a flourishing win-win. Please complete the Flourish Conversion Chart below.

STORM YOUR BRAIN
Flourish Conversions

FAILURE → **FLOURISH**

In the Eye of God, flourishing is a standard characteristic and expectation; yet, for some odd reason, we have forgotten about this innate charactorial trait, waiting to be unveiled. Here are a few examples of the power of flourishing, faith, determination, and trust in God's Divine Promises at work.

- ☐ Joseph, who ultimately became an influential governor of Egypt, was sold into slavery by his jealous, envious, and covetous brothers. Despite facing many challenges and setbacks, Joseph displays resilience, understanding, and wisdom throughout his life.

- ☐ Ruth demonstrates loyalty, courage, and faithfulness despite facing many difficult circumstances. Through her faithfulness, she ultimately finds love and security in her relationship with Boaz and becomes an ancestor of King David.

- ☐ David is described as a man after God's own heart. Despite facing many challenges and struggles throughout his life, including battles with enemies, personal failures, and family conflicts, David remains faithful to God and ultimately becomes a great King of Israel.

- ☐ Esther is described as a beautiful, courageous, and wise Queen of a Persian King. Her bravery and quick thinking saved her people from destruction and secured their safety.

Although there are more flourishing success stories in the Bible, with these four, there is no doubt about what God will do, even when the odds are stacked against you. Regardless of how life appears when *Storming Your Brain*, keep it realistic, moving forward in the Spirit of Excellence.

BRAINSTORM 6
Be Realistic

Do you keep lying to yourself? Do you lie to others because you do not want them to know the truth about you? Do you hold close to a face of pretense? Do you exaggerate the truth? Are you real with God, yourself, and others? In *Storming Your Brain*, you must be realistic with your thoughts, beliefs, desires, words, and behaviors. Why? It is wise to have good, sound information based on truth and facts, not lies and half-truths, wasting precious time.

Knowing what is real and what is not can become a challenge occasionally due to information overload by sources of deceptive measures. Being realistic helps to avoid disappointments, setbacks, frustrations, and false expectations.

When we have realistic expectations, we can make informed decisions and set appropriate goals, preparing us for challenges or obstacles. It also ensures we are not caught off guard or fall for the okey-doke. When operating rationally, we can decipher what information is useful, relevant, archivable, documentable, or discardable when *Storming The Brain*.

Some may wonder why they should strive to be realistic, primarily when they could rely on faith, trust, or hope for a miracle or the manifestation of God's Divine Plan or Will for our lives. Not realizing we must become active participants, knowing what is what and who is whom. Why? If we avoid putting in the work or Spiritually Tilling our own ground for ourselves, we will become naive, weak, and vulnerable. Because of this, the enemy sits back and waits for the right moment to take the sheep to the slaughter. Henceforth, *"Be sober, be vigilant; because your adversary the devil walks about like a roaring lion, seeking whom he may devour."* 1 Peter 5:8. Amid Spiritual Sobriety, *As It Pleases God*, we must become realistic and ready!

The value of being realistic in the Eye of God is not something to joke around with. Why? When we call upon Him or need a Legion of Angels dispatched to save us, we cannot play around with not having the Spiritual Power at our beck and call. Fake Power or Anointing is not going to get it! So, we cannot lose sight of ourselves or our Predestined Blueprint because we need the Spiritual Cover that comes with it. *"Therefore humble yourselves under the mighty hand of God, that He may exalt you in due time, casting all your care upon Him, for He cares for you."* 1 Peter 5:6-7.

Being realistic means accepting the reality of our situation without denying, avoiding, or exaggerating while acknowledging the facts, challenges, and opportunities. If we are in denial, it creates an internal blockage, allowing the psyche to dictate based on its preferences, desires, lusts, and habitual nature.

Recognizing our strengths and weaknesses, virtues and vices, gifts and talents, and limitations and potentiality makes us GREAT in the Eye of God. How? Admitting our mistakes and sins while repenting, asking for forgiveness, grace, and mercy puts our hearts in a work-in-progress status. What can this do for us? Here are a few benefits, but not limited to such:

- ☐ It helps us grow Mentally, Physically, Emotionally, and Spiritually.
- ☐ It helps us avoid self-deception and pride.
- ☐ It keeps us from thinking we are better or worse than we really are.

- ☐ It helps us avoid doing things without adding God into the equation.
- ☐ It helps prevent the despair, fear, and anxiety that lies create.
- ☐ It prevents us from becoming paralyzed from taking action or making changes.
- ☐ It keeps us from doubting God's presence and power.
- ☐ It helps us avoid complacency and indifference.
- ☐ It helps us strive for excellence or seek improvement to become better, stronger, and wiser.
- ☐ It keeps us from losing interest in God's Divine Purpose or our Predestined Blueprint.
- ☐ It helps us develop humility and gratitude.
- ☐ It helps us to share without any strings attached.
- ☐ It helps us develop courage and resilience.
- ☐ It helps us face difficulties, challenges, and overcome obstacles.
- ☐ It helps us rely on God's strength and support.
- ☐ It helps us develop wisdom and discernment.
- ☐ It helps us understand red flags.
- ☐ It helps us make good choices with sound judgments.
- ☐ It helps us Spiritually Align with God's Divine Will, *As It Pleases Him.*

Being realistic in the Eye of God is not a contradiction or a compromise. It is a way of living authentically and faithfully, honoring Him with our Mind, Body, Soul, and Spirit. When *Storming Your Brain*, here is a Realistic Conversion Chart designed to help you convert your untruths to truths.

STORM YOUR BRAIN
Realistic Conversions

UNTRUTH		TRUTH
	⋯➔	
	⋯➔	
	⋯➔	
	⋯➔	
	⋯➔	
	⋯➔	
	⋯➔	
	⋯➔	
	⋯➔	
	⋯➔	
	⋯➔	
	⋯➔	
	⋯➔	
	⋯➔	
	⋯➔	
	⋯➔	
	⋯➔	
	⋯➔	
	⋯➔	
	⋯➔	
	⋯➔	
	⋯➔	

Admit When You Are Wrong

Who enjoys admitting when they are wrong? In all transparency, we are not created to enjoy wrongfully erring; this is why God gave us a conscience to convict and help us during our Heaven on Earth Experiences. Really? Yes, really! Before going any further, here is what 1 Peter 3:16 says: *"Having a good conscience, that when they defame you as evildoers, those who revile your good conduct in Christ may be ashamed."*

For our sake, admitting, taking responsibility for our actions, and apologizing are liberating in the Eye of God, and it is also humbling because it takes courage to admit we are wrong. Plus, it ultimately leads to personal growth and better outcomes without continually compounding lies, having to remember the previous lie we told, or pointing the finger to shift blame. James 5:16 states, *"Confess your trespasses to one another, and pray for one another, that you may be healed. The effective, fervent prayer of a righteous man avails much."*

A willingness to authentically learn and grow, *As It Pleases God*, requires us to admit our mistakes. Why? First, it symbolically filters our conscience as a sign of strength, not weakness. Secondly, it opens the door to insight and constructive feedback, helping build a stronger relationship with God, ourselves, and others, in this Divine Order. Thirdly, acknowledging our errors can prevent future mistakes and improve our decision-making or brainstorming skills without whitewashing. 1 John 1:9 says, *"If we confess our sins, He is faithful and just to forgive us our sins and to cleanse us from all unrighteousness."*

What if we are not wrong? Do we still take responsibility? If we are not wrong, there is no need to take responsibility, apologize, or entertain foolery. In Matthew 5:11, Jesus teaches, *"Blessed are you when they revile and persecute you, and say all kinds of evil against you falsely for My sake."* However, considering other perspectives and being open to feedback is always essential. Why? We are always on a learning curve, so there may be opportunities for growth, learning, and improvement, even if we are not in the wrong. It is also essential to maintain a humble and respectful attitude towards others, regardless of whether we are right, wrong, or indifferent, using the Fruits of the Spirit as Divine Leverage.

On the other hand, to de-escalate an issue, sometimes it is only wise to offer an apology and move on in the Spirit of Excellence. Why is an apology necessary? For the sake of peace, I would extend an apology and change the conversational topic, becoming the bigger person and diffusing the tension to create a more positive, productive, and fruitful environment for everyone involved. Why? In the Kingdom of God, it is WISE to take responsibility for any mistakes, misclarifications, or misunderstandings that may have occurred and to show empathy towards the other person's feelings.

While some individuals may perceive apologizing as a sign of weakness, it is a strong people skill quality that makes us pristinely top-notch in the Eye of God. How? By taking responsibility for our actions, thoughts, words, and reactions while showing empathy toward others, we demonstrate maturity and a willingness to improve ourselves and our relationships with trust and respect for all.

BRAINSTORM 7
Learn Something New

Are you on a learning curve? Do you enjoy learning something new? Do you despise change? Are you complacent? When *Storming Your Brain*, learning something new is crucial for your growth, development, and maturity. You can expand your capacity beyond measure by adding God into your equational learning efforts. Is this Biblical? Absolutely. Proverbs 1:7 says, *"The fear of the Lord is the beginning of knowledge, but fools despise wisdom and instruction."* In light of this, you must start somewhere, so it may as well be here and now.

Expanding our mental capacity in or out of the Kingdom of God is necessary to stimulate our brain cells. If they are not stimulated, they will begin to die off, as if they have no use for hanging around. Whereas all hope is not lost, according to the Heavenly of Heavens, we can stimulate the growth of new cells to cater to our Predestined Blueprint. What does this mean? When we put a reason behind the stimulation for the greater good, such as *Storming The Brain*, it will generate more of what we need to facilitate the intended purpose, especially when it is DIVINE.

We can create anything our heart desires when broadening our knowledge, expanding our skills, and enhancing our problem-solving abilities. Nevertheless, according to our Blueprinted Mission, we must keep our minds active and engaged. Why? It improves our cognitive function and mental agility. In so many words, it keeps our mental wheels turning in the right direction, especially in a rapidly changing world with groundbreaking technology.

What if we are tired of learning? It is okay to rest occasionally; however, we cannot stop altogether. We are prewired to learn, grow, and sow back into the Kingdom of God when called upon; therefore, we must be ready, willing, and able to do what we are called to do. If one does not know their reason for being, it is time to *Learn Something New*. What is that? The other side of you!

Learning Something New is a MINDSET. I have a chart below to help assist in the different ways of categorizing learning. What is categorized learning? It is a sort of learning that prevents tunnel vision, allowing us to glean from everything and everyone without limiting our mental capacity.

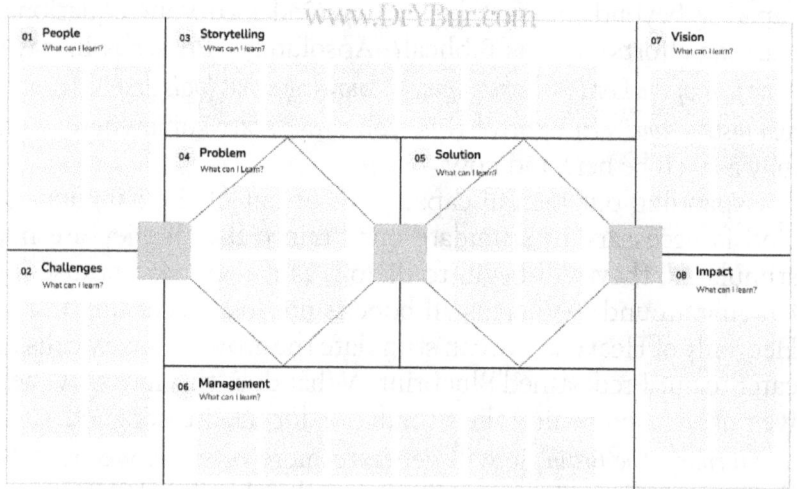

What is the purpose of this chart? It gets us into the habit of documenting what we learned and did not, what we need to learn, why we need to learn, and how to do so. Besides, when we seek answers from God, it may not be packaged as we envision. For this reason, we must open our brainiac mind to download information, leaving no stone unturned. For example, if we have an adult issue, He may send the answer through a child, animal, tree, or whatever. Therefore, when *Storming The Brain*, we must stay on READY with pen and paper.

According to the Heavenly of Heavens, we must acquire knowledge, and once we get an understanding, we must seek more to add to what we already possess. Proverbs 18:15 says, *"The heart of the prudent acquires knowledge, and the ear of the wise seeks knowledge."* Compounded knowledge leads to wisdom. By adding God into the equation, they become Divine Wisdom, the reason behind *The WHY Blueprint*. What does this mean? The goal is to get to the DIVINE status with a READYROLL Blueprint, *As It Pleases God*. Why? It does not make sense to continue to walk around clueless about our reason for being; it is time to step up to the plate and hit a home run.

Everything we ever wanted and dreamed about is hidden within our ability to *Learn Something New* without judgment of how God delivers it. Why is this so important? Unfortunately, the typical reason we do not obtain our heart's desire is due to the fact that we unawaringly judge the answer, solution, or meal ticket, putting tangibles over intangibles. Really? Yes, really! Whatever you *Storm Your Brain* to learn, it is WISE to add God into your equational efforts. It makes the gleaning process easier, more understandable, and intrinsically relatable. Here is the Spiritual Seal: *"And whatever you do, do it heartily, as to the Lord and not to men, knowing that from the Lord you will receive the reward of the inheritance; for you serve the Lord Christ."* Colossians 3:23-24. Whenever you *Learn Something New*, make sure you document it.

STORM YOUR BRAIN
New Learning List

- [ ] What Do I Need To Learn?
- [ ] What Do I Need To Learn?
- [ ] What Do I Need To Learn?
- [ ] What Do I Need To Learn?
- [ ] What Do I Need To Learn?
- [ ] What Do I Need To Learn?
- [ ] What Do I Need To Learn?
- [ ] What Do I Need To Learn?
- [ ] What Do I Need To Learn?
- [ ] What Do I Need To Learn?
- [ ] What Do I Need To Learn?
- [ ] What Do I Need To Learn?
- [ ] What Do I Need To Learn?
- [ ] What Do I Need To Learn?
- [ ] What Do I Need To Learn?
- [ ] What Do I Need To Learn?

STORM YOUR BRAIN
New Learning List

- [ ] What Do I Need To Learn?
- [ ] What Do I Need To Learn?
- [ ] What Do I Need To Learn?
- [ ] What Do I Need To Learn?
- [ ] What Do I Need To Learn?
- [ ] What Do I Need To Learn?
- [ ] What Do I Need To Learn?
- [ ] What Do I Need To Learn?
- [ ] What Do I Need To Learn?
- [ ] What Do I Need To Learn?
- [ ] What Do I Need To Learn?
- [ ] What Do I Need To Learn?
- [ ] What Do I Need To Learn?
- [ ] What Do I Need To Learn?
- [ ] What Do I Need To Learn?
- [ ] What Do I Need To Learn?

STORM YOUR BRAIN
New Learning List

- [ ] What Do I Need To Learn?
- [ ] What Do I Need To Learn?
- [ ] What Do I Need To Learn?
- [ ] What Do I Need To Learn?
- [ ] What Do I Need To Learn?
- [ ] What Do I Need To Learn?
- [ ] What Do I Need To Learn?
- [ ] What Do I Need To Learn?
- [ ] What Do I Need To Learn?
- [ ] What Do I Need To Learn?
- [ ] What Do I Need To Learn?
- [ ] What Do I Need To Learn?
- [ ] What Do I Need To Learn?
- [ ] What Do I Need To Learn?
- [ ] What Do I Need To Learn?
- [ ] What Do I Need To Learn?

BRAINSTORM 8

Let Go

Today's most prominent question is, 'How do we let go?' 'When should we let go?' 'Why should we let go?' Letting go is one of the hardest things to do, yet the most important. According to the Heavenly of Heavens, this tug-of-war must stop! The pulling and tugging Mentally, Physically, Emotionally, Spiritually, and Financially must be converted into a state of peace with an understanding, *"All things work together for good to those who love God, to those who are the called according to His purpose."* Romans 8:28. If we are not in Purpose on purpose, it is time to do something about it.

We cannot continue to hold on to our own agenda, past mistakes, traumas, unforgiveness, shame, abandonment, and regrets. We must let go to Spiritually Grow, *As It Pleases God.* When *Storming The Brain*, the burden is too heavy to carry alone. Why? It weighs the brain down. By learning from your mistakes and focusing on the present moment, you can free yourself from the negative emotions holding you back from using your highest and greatest potential.

No one is exempt from making mistakes and experiencing setbacks, but how we respond to these challenges ultimately defines, trains, and propels us. Instead of dwelling on the past, focus on the opportunities and possibilities ahead. What makes this so important in the Eye of God? By letting go of past mistakes and regrets, you can open your mind and *Storm Your Brain* to become better, stronger, and wiser, *As It Pleases Him*, instead of pleasing yourself.

I am not discounting anyone's past experiences because it is indeed our past that forms who we are, positively or negatively. I get it...letting go of our past can be a complex and emotional process, but it is an essential step towards moving forward with our Predestined Blueprint in hand. Here are some tips that may help in *Storming The Brain* or *Letting Go*, but are not limited to such:

1. **Step One**: We must accept that our past is a part of us as a formal training ground to shape and propel us into Divine Greatness. Acknowledging the pain, hurt, disappointments, setbacks, or mistakes is a part of the healing process. Still, we must also learn to accept them and move forward positively in the Spirit of Excellence with the LESSONS and Testimonies in hand.

2. **Step Two**: Forgiving ourselves and others for wrongdoings is crucial to letting go of our past. Holding onto anger and resentment hinders our ability to move forward, find peace, or *Storm The Brain* properly. Unforgiveness is invisible handcuffs that we have the key to. Really? Yes, really! Forgiveness is the key to releasing us. God has given us the Spiritual Tool of Forgiveness to release the psyche, and we are responsible for using it.

3. **Step Three**: Focus on the positive aspects of our past and become GRATEFUL for the lessons learned. This reverential process can help shift our perspective, releasing the negative emotions associated with it.

4. **Step Four**: Taking care of ourselves Physically, Mentally, Emotionally, Spiritually, and Financially is vital for

moving forward. This regimen may include seeking therapy, practicing mindfulness, taking self-help classes, reading our Bibles, or engaging in activities that bring us joy. All of these help us overcome selfishness, pridefulness, and dullness to maximize the Fruits of the Spirit and exhibit Christlike Character.

Remember, Psalm 37:23-24 says, *"The steps of a good man are ordered by the Lord, and He delights in his way. Though he fall, he shall not be utterly cast down; for the Lord upholds him with His hand."*

Expectations

Letting go of false expectations can be difficult, but it can also be incredibly liberating. When we hold onto self-created expectations, we set ourselves up for disappointment. Why? We feel let down when we create a rigid idea of how we want things to be, and when they do not pan out exactly as we imagined, disappointment grips the psyche with depression, stress, anger, fear, worry, or anxiety. Unfortunately, the more it happens, the tighter the grip becomes.

On the other hand, when we embrace Spiritual Alignment, *As It Pleases God*, we open ourselves up to new possibilities, understanding, training, and experiences. In the Eye of God, adaptability and flexibility can help us easily navigate the Cycles and Vicissitudes of Life without getting stuck in the cycle of déjà vu. How can we streamline our false expectations with the Will of God? We must SEEK the meaning of our being and the unveiling of our Divine Blueprint. With this knowledge, it becomes easier to *Let Go* of the foolery designed to circumvent our Divine Destiny. Without this knowledge, we become susceptible to recklessness. What does this mean? The falsified odds are stacked against those who DO NOT know their Divine Purpose compared to those who do.

How can we change our mindset toward our expectations of ourselves and others? We must redirect everything and everyone back to God Almighty, *As It Pleases Him.* How? It will vary from person to person, situation to situation, trauma to trauma, culture to culture, and so on. However, for *Storming The Brain*, here are a few basics, but not limited to such:

- Develop a *Spirit to Spirit* Relationship with God, our Heavenly Father.
- Cover ourselves with the Blood of Jesus as Spiritual Atonement.
- Awaken our Spirit to become ONE with the Holy Spirit to guide, nurture, teach, and help us.
- Pray, repent, and forgive ourselves and others.
- Use the Fruits of the Spirit (Love, Joy, Peace, Patience, Kindness, Goodness, Faithfulness, Gentleness, and Self-Control).
- Behave Christlike, exuding pristine people skills.
- Use the Word of God to align, teach, navigate, correct, and inspire.
- Speak positively, counteract all negativity as much as possible, and shut down negative, unproductive, or unfruitful self-talk or random chatter.
- Govern the mind with positive, productive, and fruitful thoughts.
- Eliminate jealousy, envy, pride, greed, coveting, competitiveness, and debauchery.
- Repeat consistently, "*I can do all things through Christ who strengthens me.*" Philippians 4:13.

Now, my question is, 'What do you need to *Let Go of*?' Please complete the *Let Go Chart*, documenting the answers.

STORM YOUR BRAIN
Let Go List

- [ ] What Do You Need To Let Go?
- [ ] What Do You Need To Let Go?
- [ ] What Do You Need To Let Go?
- [ ] What Do You Need To Let Go?
- [ ] What Do You Need To Let Go?
- [ ] What Do You Need To Let Go?
- [ ] What Do You Need To Let Go?
- [ ] What Do You Need To Let Go?
- [ ] What Do You Need To Let Go?
- [ ] What Do You Need To Let Go?
- [ ] What Do You Need To Let Go?
- [ ] What Do You Need To Let Go?
- [ ] What Do You Need To Let Go?
- [ ] What Do You Need To Let Go?
- [ ] What Do You Need To Let Go?
- [ ] What Do You Need To Let Go?

Storming The Brain is an excellent Spiritual Tool we do not want to live without. Why? Being able to challenge our mind, *As It Pleases God*, creates an unprecedented Spiritual Alliance with the Heavenly of Heavens on our behalf. So, it behooves us to eliminate the toxicity as much as possible to keep our Spiritual Channels of Divine Communication open.

BRAINSTORM 9
Cultivating Growth

Are you ready to grow? Has your growth become stunted? Have you maxed out your growth spurt? Do you think you know everything you need to know about life and God Almighty? Well, there is more...and the Heavenly of Heavens has placed a Divine Decree to *Storm Your Brain*. Why? We are NOT maximizing our Spiritual Growth Potential, *As It Pleases Him*.

Cultivating Growth is a Spiritual Refining Process that uses our basic knowledge, skills, and perspectives as preparatory training to build the Kingdom of God and feed His sheep. Why? We must be Spiritually Equipped before being Spiritually Commissioned. In other words, we must embrace challenges, learn from failures, and seek feedback to improve ourselves from the inside out. According to the Heavenly of Heavens, it helps us become more resilient, imaginative, teachable, and adaptable when using our Spiritual Gifts, Calling, Talents, Creativity, and Know-How, *As It Pleases God*.

What if we are already Spiritually Equipped and feeding God's sheep? Congratulations. Then my question would be, 'Are you using the Fruits of the Spirit?' 'Do you know your reason for being?' 'Do you have your Divine Blueprint documented?' 'Do you know how to *Storm Your Brain*?' If not, once again, there is MORE!

Many Believers have approached me, proclaiming they are the Chosen One, as if God has not chosen others. Yet, they proceeded to hit me over the head with the Bible, as if I were clueless about the Word of God. Why would they persist with the HELLBOUND approach? I was diligently holding my tongue to see how far to the left they would take the Word of God. Plus, I wanted to see how long it would take the Holy Spirit to reveal what they should have known. What does this mean? Spirit knows Spirit!

The bottom line is that they should have perceived something when proclaiming to be a Chosen One. If they did not, it meant their Spiritual Growth was stunted. Therefore, they should not have bragged about their Spiritual Status because I will hold them accountable and TEST the Spirit. Why would I test the Spirit? First, it should have been something they should have done before approaching me or making a proclamation about their Spiritual Status. Secondly, I must protect my Spiritual Anointing from the wolves in sheep's clothing. Thirdly, I must know which Spiritual Fruits to use to protect my Christlike Posture.

The authentic Chosen Ones from the Heavenly of Heavens do not broadcast their Spiritual Status. Why? Bragging is a worldly attribute! Those who know who is whom in the Realm of the Spirit know, and those who do not know will not, but humility is required. What does this mean in layman's terms? If we are CHOSEN, we know it; therefore, we do not need to announce it or convince anyone. Our responsibility is to REMAIN upright, *As It Pleases God*. Please allow me to Spiritually Align accordingly: *"So you may walk in the way of goodness, And keep to the paths of righteousness. For the upright will dwell in the land, And the blameless will remain in it; But the wicked will be cut off from the earth, And the unfaithful will be uprooted from it."* Proverbs 2:20-22.

Storming The Brain with a REMAIN mindset can potentially increase our fruits, Spiritual Fruits, to be exact. According to the

Heavenly of Heavens, we must know: "*Until the Spirit is poured upon us from on high, And the wilderness becomes a fruitful field, And the fruitful field is counted as a forest. Then justice will dwell in the wilderness, And righteousness remain in the fruitful field. The work of righteousness will be peace, And the effect of righteousness, quietness and assurance forever. My people will dwell in a peaceful habitation, In secure dwellings, and in quiet resting places.*" Isaiah 32:15-18.

When *Cultivating Growth*, the keyword is to PERCEIVE, similar to how Eli perceives the Lord calling Samuel in 1 Samuel 3. What is the big deal about our ability to perceive? If we do not perceive correctly, it alerts us that something is keeled or our Spiritual Compass is off; therefore, we must seek corrective measures to pinpoint the issue.

More importantly, God despises the actions of those who perceive and decree from their own hearts, leaving Him out of the equation. What is the big deal? Instead of *Storming The Brain* to Spiritually Download *As it Pleases God*, we will get a self-induced whirlwind Mentally, Physically, Emotionally, Spiritually, or Financially.

What is the purpose of inducing a whirlwind in our lives, especially when we are Believers and feeding God's sheep? First, there is a big difference in *Cultivating Growth*, according to Kingdom Standards, rather than our own. Secondly, feeding His sheep how we see fit will not get it, especially in the Eye of God. Thirdly, when *Storming The Brain*, we cannot expect the Heavenly of Heavens to download Divine Information when we are hellbent on doing our own or the wrong thing. Fourthly, when we use the Word of God to manipulate or browbeat others without upping the ante on our *Spirit to Spirit* communicative efforts, we will create a self-induced tizzy. Lastly, without using the Fruits of the Spirit and behaving Christlike, *As It Pleases Him*, disobedience, dullness, and stiff necks will cause us to get a Spiritual Side-Eye.

How can we make this make sense, primarily when we have free will, grace, and mercy working for us? According to our Predestined Blueprint, we cannot use them as an excuse for not cultivating our own growth or missing the mark. Nor can we use them to mislead others in His Divine Name, catering to our own agenda. Is this Biblical? I would have it no other way! *"They continually say to those who despise Me, the LORD has said, 'You shall have peace.' And to everyone who walks according to the dictates of his own heart, they say, 'No evil shall come upon you.' For who has stood in the counsel of the LORD, And has perceived and heard His word? Who has marked His word and heard it? Behold, a whirlwind of the LORD has gone forth in fury—A violent whirlwind! It will fall violently on the head of the wicked. The anger of the LORD will not turn back Until He has executed and performed the thoughts of His heart. In the latter days you will understand it perfectly. 'I have not sent these prophets, yet they ran. I have not spoken to them, yet they prophesied.'"* Jeremiah 23:17-21.

When *Cultivating Growth*, we must seek to unveil our Predestined Blueprint instead of barking up the wrong tree, hoping, praying, and wishing it is the right one. How do we know if it is the right one? We must consistently add God into our equational efforts, seeking Him, *Spirit to Spirit*, with pen and paper ready to document.

When *Storming Your Brain*, repeat this: *"Speak, LORD, for Your servant hears."* 1 Samuel 3:10. Why? It lets God know that you are open to receiving Divine Information. Once you become consistent with this process and document accordingly, He will *Storm Your Brain* like never before, guaranteed!

STORM YOUR BRAIN
Cultivating List

- [ ] What Needs Cultivating?
- [ ] What Needs Cultivating?
- [ ] What Needs Cultivating?
- [ ] What Needs Cultivating?
- [ ] What Needs Cultivating?
- [ ] What Needs Cultivating?
- [ ] What Needs Cultivating?
- [ ] What Needs Cultivating?
- [ ] What Needs Cultivating?
- [ ] What Needs Cultivating?
- [ ] What Needs Cultivating?
- [ ] What Needs Cultivating?
- [ ] What Needs Cultivating?
- [ ] What Needs Cultivating?
- [ ] What Needs Cultivating?
- [ ] What Needs Cultivating?
- [ ] What Needs Cultivating?

www.DrYBur.com

BRAINSTORM 10

Consistency

Are you consistent? Are you always late? Do you lose track of time? Do you respect the time of another? Do you feel wishy-washy at times? As a Badge of Honor in *The WHY Blueprint*, practicing self-discipline and consistency is essential.

On the other hand, when *Storming The Brain*, they are MANDATORY. Why are they so important? They help us stay committed to achieving our desires, goals, values, and Predestined Blueprint. By setting clear boundaries and sticking to them, we can avoid frivolous distractions that break our focus on what truly matters. Consistency also helps us build good habits and stay accountable to God, ourselves, and others.

Practicing self-discipline and consistency, *As It Pleases God*, builds our trust, faith, hope, and reliance on Him with a Spiritual Relationship of interdependency. By avoiding developing a relationship as such, we will find ourselves all over the place, giving in to the next quick fix with the illusion of more power, money, and sex. If the lust of the eyes, the lusts of the flesh, and the pride of life are not tamed or on a leash, we will become drawn away to unfavorable conditions in the Eye of God.

For example, when someone proclaims to be prosperous and highly favored by God with or without deep pockets, I look for consistency and self-discipline. Why? God will use anyone or anything to accomplish His Divine Will; however, it is a different story when proclaiming the Favor of God. What does this mean? Just because we appear better off than others does not mean we are in Purpose on purpose, nor does it mean we know our reason for being. We cannot equate tangibles with intangibles when dealing with God Almighty.

With or without tangibles, God wants to know what we will do about the insatiable longing from within. What is the big deal? The longing from within the psyche is there for a reason. If we do not become consistent in understanding it, *As It Pleases Him*, it becomes an imploding or exploding PIT, causing us to do things we never thought we were capable of doing. Really? Yes, really!

Most of those who are behind bars are there due to unresolved issues and traumas associated with the lust of the eyes, the lusts of the flesh, and the pride of life, with a longing for the Fruits of the Spirit. If someone had consistently taken the time to exhibit the Fruits of the Spirit (Love, Joy, Peace, Patience, Kindness, Goodness, Faithfulness, Gentleness, and Self-Control) and Christlike Character when they were younger, it could have changed the trajectory of their lives.

Then again, it is impossible to intervene if we do not know how to use the Fruits of the Spirit or share them, *As It Pleases God*. As a result, we do our best, but is it good enough in the Eye of God? In *Storming The Brain*, we want to eliminate the 'What if' factors associated with feeding God's sheep by knowing our consistencies and inconsistencies. Please complete the charts below.

STORM YOUR BRAIN
Consistency List

- [ ] Where Am I Consistent?
- [ ] Where Am I Consistent?
- [ ] Where Am I Consistent?
- [ ] Where Am I Consistent?
- [ ] Where Am I Consistent?
- [ ] Where Am I Consistent?
- [ ] Where Am I Consistent?
- [ ] Where Am I Consistent?
- [ ] Where Am I Consistent?
- [ ] Where Am I Consistent?
- [ ] Where Am I Consistent?
- [ ] Where Am I Consistent?
- [ ] Where Am I Consistent?
- [ ] Where Am I Consistent?
- [ ] Where Am I Consistent?
- [ ] Where Am I Consistent?

STORM YOUR BRAIN
Inconsistency List

- [ ] Where Am I Inconsistent?
- [ ] Where Am I Inconsistent?
- [ ] Where Am I Inconsistent?
- [ ] Where Am I Inconsistent?
- [ ] Where Am I Inconsistent?
- [ ] Where Am I Inconsistent?
- [ ] Where Am I Inconsistent?
- [ ] Where Am I Inconsistent?
- [ ] Where Am I Inconsistent?
- [ ] Where Am I Inconsistent?
- [ ] Where Am I Inconsistent?
- [ ] Where Am I Inconsistent?
- [ ] Where Am I Inconsistent?
- [ ] Where Am I Inconsistent?
- [ ] Where Am I Inconsistent?
- [ ] Where Am I Inconsistent?

Why must we know our consistencies and inconsistencies? We must know our areas of wavering, especially in our faith, hope, trust, and love. *"Let us hold fast the confession of our hope without wavering, for He who promised is faithful."* Hebrews 10:23.

Divine Favor from the Heavenly of Heavens comes with a Spiritual Classroom requiring discipline, self-control, and humility. So when someone claims to be at a specific Spiritual Level and swings it high and low, they cannot control their tongue, they exhibit atrocious behavior, and do everything with a combative Spirit with rotten fruits all over the place, I already know their loyalty is not 100% for the Kingdom. Why? We all have consistency, but the question remains, 'What are we consistent with, or to whom?'

Some would say, 'I was born inconsistent.' According to the Heavenly of Heavens, this is not a factual statement, even if we are convinced it is. Consistency with the Kingdom of God exists within our DNA, especially if we make it from the Realm of the Spirit into the earthly realm. Therefore, it must be redirected back to the Kingdom to become Spiritually Aligned, *As It Pleases God*.

Although we take the Breath of Life for granted, it means something in the Realm of the Spirit. What does it mean? If we are breathing, we still have a Divine Mission and work to do for the Kingdom of God. Even if our Predestined Blueprint is hidden in plain sight, it does not mean we should not seek to unveil or protect it. What should we do? Work on it consistently, *Spirit to Spirit* with our Heavenly Father.

What if we cannot hear God? If we can hear ourselves speak, we can hear God. If we can entertain negative thoughts, we can hear God. If we can cuss someone out without saying one word, we can hear God. If we can think or fantasize about someone or something, we can hear God. It is often said, 'Where there is a will, there is a way!'

In *Storming The Brain*, we do not settle for excuses or engage in pointing the finger to shift responsibility. We believe that setting boundaries for self-discipline and consistency is wisdom in the making. This process involves a few items, but is not limited to such:

- ☐ Align ourselves with the Holy Trinity (The Father, Son, and Holy Spirit).
- ☐ Identify what is essential and what is not, getting rid of tomfoolery.
- ☐ Determine what we want to achieve and why.
- ☐ Set and document clear goals.
- ☐ Create a plan of action, mind map, or roadmap.
- ☐ Determine and understand our Calling, Talents, Creativity, and Purpose.
- ☐ Determine the skills or the know-how needed to stay on track.
- ☐ Identify potential distractions.
- ☐ Understand our strengths and weaknesses.
- ☐ Establish rules for managing the Mind, Body, Soul, and Spirit with relevancy and the Word of God.

What if we do not exercise self-discipline or consistency? Without them, we may struggle, feel lost, experience regret, feel unfulfilled, unsatisfied, and clueless about what we are doing and why. Meanwhile, we will depend on others to fill a void that only God can Spiritually Seal due to unresolved stress and anxiety. What if they are our weakness? We must identify underlying seeds, roots, and fruits associated with these issues by *Storming The Brain*. Besides, they may be a hidden strength in disguise underneath an apparent weakness; therefore, we must leave no stone unturned.

We must become disciplined and consistent in understanding our weaknesses. Here is a Stone Turning Chart.

STONE TURNING CHART

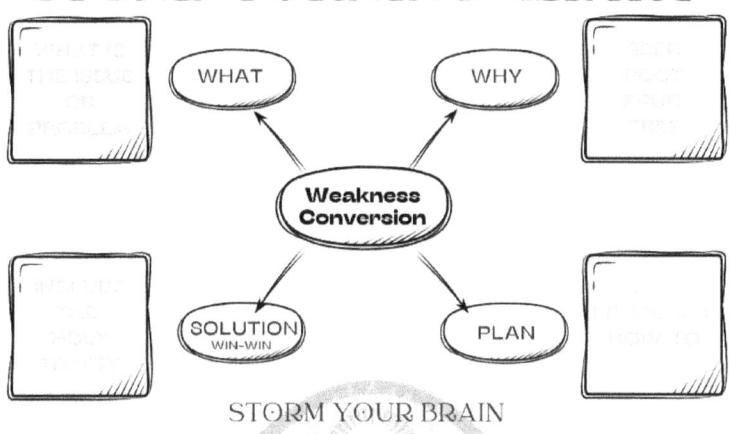

Every weakness I possessed was a hidden strength; had I left the stone unturned, there would not be *The WHY Blueprint*, *Build Your Own Table*, *Storm Your Brain*, or the *As It Pleases God*® Movement.

BRAINSTORM 11
Tug-of-War of Beliefs

Are you caught between a rock and a hard place? Are you secretly or openly fighting against yourself and others? Is the tug-of-war within your psyche becoming stronger than you? If you do not know why you do what you do, why are you doing it?

Cluelessness about our beliefs creates a domino effect, causing us to placate negativity, which depletes our brain cells. Unfortunately, this is NOT a joke. Due to negative conditioning or culture, those brainwashed, exhibiting a negative belief system, or in a cycle of tug-of-war, usually do not realize their harmful or toxic condition.

Adaptation is real. If the mind adapts to a specific belief system or way of life, it can become challenging to deprogram someone who does not understand that there is a programming issue unless God intervenes. Why? We have free will to believe how we desire because we are not robots; therefore, in the Kingdom of God, we must respect others, even if we disagree.

Regardless of our feelings or beliefs, we must want God and become a part of the Kingdom for ourselves. If we become cultish with our approach, we are no better than a manipulator straight out of the PIT. Blasphemy, right? Wrong. *"The Lord has appeared of* old to me, saying: 'Yes, I have loved you with an everlasting love; Therefore with lovingkindness I have drawn you.' " Jeremiah 31:3.

Mental cleansing is necessary to break free of a chained, doomed, and gloomy mindset. God wants us to operate with the Fruits of the Spirit and behave Christlike without traumatizing others in His Name, as if He is causing us to misbehave. What should we do? When we are in a *Tug-of-War of Beliefs*, James 4:8 says in layman's terms, "*Draw near to God and He will draw near to you. Cleanse your hands, you sinners; and purify your hearts, you double-minded.*"

Why does challenging the *Tug-of-War of Beliefs* and assumptions need revamping in the Eye of God? They can lead to harmful thoughts, actions, reactions, biases, stereotypes, and debauchery toward ourselves and others. In addition, we can better understand Kingdom Expectations and worldly ones by questioning our beliefs and examining where they come from and why. Then again, understanding 1 Corinthians 6:19-20 can change the trajectory of our lives. It says, "*Do you not know that your body is the temple of the Holy Spirit who is in you, whom you have from God, and you are not your own? For you were bought at a price; therefore glorify God in your body and in your spirit, which are God's.*"

Whether in a *Tug-of-War of Beliefs* or not, we belong to God. Every living being belongs to Him, and everything else He created belongs to Him. Once we begin to RESPECT these Spiritual Factors, we can effectively challenge our beliefs and assumptions, *As It Pleases Him*. Without respect, we will fall into a selfish category, depleting our rights to remove the Spiritual Scales, keeping us Divinely Blind, Deaf, and Mute to the abundance flowing from the Heavenly of Heavens.

What do Spiritual Scales mean? With all due respect, this analogy is similar to the scales on a fish. Why would I use a slimy, smelly fish when comparing a Spiritual Principle out of all the other animals on the face of this earth? Fortunately, a fish would be a relevant depiction of getting my point across effectively. How so? Simply put, the word SELFISH contains the word fish! Being that we are on a constant selling curve, positively or negatively, the fish scales are deemed appropriate until we become SELFLESS in the Eye of God.

Here is the deal: We cannot get to the meat without removing the scales on a fish, right? The same applies to the Realm of the Spirit; the Spiritual Scales must be removed to get to the Spiritual Meat of the Kingdom. If not, we will remain on Spiritual Milk, in a cycle of déjà vu with the same o' same o' with different characters, sucking the life out of us.

What is the big deal as long as we get God's Word? We are required to GROW and sow back into the Kingdom when called upon! And if we are still suckling, we will not be ready for the unveiling of our Blueprinted Purpose. Is this Biblical? I would have it no other way. *"For though by this time you ought to be teachers, you need someone to teach you again the first principles of the oracles of God; and you have come to need milk and not solid food. For everyone who partakes only of milk is unskilled in the word of righteousness, for he is a babe."* Hebrews 5:12-13.

In the Eye of God, we must approach this challenging process with an open mind and a willingness to learn and grow instead of trying to defend our negative or debauched beliefs. Why? If we are not operating in the Fruits of the Spirit and behaving Christlike, we are already operating in a Spiritual Deficit. Blasphemy, right? Wrong. Please allow me to Spiritually Align: *"And I, brethren, could not speak to you as to spiritual people but as to carnal, as to babes in Christ. I fed you with milk and not with solid food; for until now you were not able to receive it, and even now you are still not able."* 1 Corinthians 3:1-2. When we try to defend or justify our negative beliefs, we are less likely to open ourselves up to new information or perspectives challenging them, *As It Pleases God*. Unfortunately, this can lead to a closed or reprobate mind, limiting our ability to learn, grow, or *Storm The Brain* properly.

What if we refuse to challenge our negative belief system? Once again, we have free will to change for the better or refuse to remain where we are in our selfish or self-willed ways. Here is what Romans 1:28-32 says, *"And even as they did not like to retain God in their knowledge, God gave them over to a debased mind, to do those things which are not fitting; being filled with all unrighteousness, sexual immorality, wickedness, covetousness, maliciousness; full of envy, murder, strife, deceit, evil-mindedness; they are whisperers, backbiters, haters of God, violent, proud, boasters, inventors of evil things, disobedient to parents, undiscerning, untrustworthy, unloving, unforgiving, unmerciful; who, knowing the righteous judgment of God, that those who practice such things are deserving of death, not only do the same but also approve of those who practice them."*

What can we do differently? *"Repent, and turn from all your transgressions, so that iniquity will not be your ruin."* Ezekiel 18:30b. We must also be willing to question and examine ourselves, *As It Pleases God*, allowing Him to expand our understanding from His Divine Perspective. Here is what the Bible says about self-examination: *"Examine yourselves as to whether you are in the faith. Test yourselves. Do you not know yourselves, that Jesus Christ is in you? — unless indeed you are disqualified."* 2 Corinthians 13:5. How do we convert our negative *Tug-of-War Beliefs*? First, we must know and take responsibility for what they are and what they are not. Secondly, we must know our positive beliefs. And thirdly, we must move from selfishness to *As It Pleases God*, using the Fruits of the Spirit. Please complete the Belief Conversion and Responsibility Chart. It will help you *Storm Your Brain*, especially when dealing with Kingdom Principles, Protocols, and Systems.

STORM YOUR BRAIN
Beliefs Conversion

NEGATIVE BELIEF		POSITIVE BELIEF
_____	⋯⟩	_____
_____	⋯⟩	_____
_____	⋯⟩	_____
_____	⋯⟩	_____
_____	⋯⟩	_____
_____	⋯⟩	_____
_____	⋯⟩	_____
_____	⋯⟩	_____
_____	⋯⟩	_____
_____	⋯⟩	_____
_____	⋯⟩	_____
_____	⋯⟩	_____
_____	⋯⟩	_____
_____	⋯⟩	_____
_____	⋯⟩	_____
_____	⋯⟩	_____
_____	⋯⟩	_____
_____	⋯⟩	_____
_____	⋯⟩	_____
_____	⋯⟩	_____
_____	⋯⟩	_____
_____	⋯⟩	_____

STORM YOUR BRAIN
Responsibility List

- [ ] Where Do I Need To Take Responsibility?
- [ ] Where Do I Need To Take Responsibility?
- [ ] Where Do I Need To Take Responsibility?
- [ ] Where Do I Need To Take Responsibility?
- [ ] Where Do I Need To Take Responsibility?
- [ ] Where Do I Need To Take Responsibility?
- [ ] Where Do I Need To Take Responsibility?
- [ ] Where Do I Need To Take Responsibility?
- [ ] Where Do I Need To Take Responsibility?
- [ ] Where Do I Need To Take Responsibility?
- [ ] Where Do I Need To Take Responsibility?
- [ ] Where Do I Need To Take Responsibility?
- [ ] Where Do I Need To Take Responsibility?
- [ ] Where Do I Need To Take Responsibility?
- [ ] Where Do I Need To Take Responsibility?
- [ ] Where Do I Need To Take Responsibility?

BRAINSTORM 12
Progress, Not Perfection

Are you positively progressing? Are you in a state of regression? Do you have a plan? Are you just going with the flow, and whatever happens, happens? Are you operating in the Spirit of Perfection? Are you operating in the Spirit of Excellence? Are you a work-in-progress? Are you operating with a Positive Mental Mindset? As I *Storm Your Brain* with many questions, the goal is to get your mental wheels turning in the right direction.

I am Dr. Y. for a reason, and I bombard the human brain and psyche with many soul-searching questions, provoking our animalistic release. Why the animalistic release? Are we not humans? Absolutely! For the record, I am not calling anyone an animal; we are discussing valuable Spiritual Principles, enabling us to *Storm The Brain* without having negative pushback.

The Bible parallels us with animals to keep us from thinking we are perfect, uncorrectable, or untouchable. Really? Yes, really! "I said in my heart, 'God shall judge the righteous and the wicked, For there is a time there for every purpose and for every work.' I said in my heart, 'Concerning the condition of the sons of men, God tests them, that they may see that they themselves are like animals.' For what happens to the sons of men also happens to animals; one thing befalls them: as one dies, so dies the other.

Surely, they all have one breath; man has no advantage over animals, for all is vanity. All go to one place: all are from the dust, and all return to dust." Ecclesiastes 3:17-20.

Although we are not from the same seed, we have a symbolic bonding relationship with animals; therefore, we have an animalistic nature if not tamed. How do we Spiritually Bond with animals? The Bible says, *"A righteous man regards the life of his animal, But the tender mercies of the wicked are cruel. He who tills his land will be satisfied with bread, But he who follows frivolity is devoid of understanding."* Proverbs 12:10-11. Animals do not have the luxury of becoming complacent, not learning, or being devoid of serving us in some capacity for our benefit. It would be unfortunate if the shoe were on the other foot, having to serve animals, right?

In the Old Testament, animals were used as burnt offerings to cover our sins and complacency. More importantly, God used them for a reason. What is the reason? For us, His chosen people! The ones who were created in His Divine Image. And what do we do? We abuse the Divine System set in place to save humanity while pretending to be perfect without working on our flawed nature.

And now that we have the Blood of Jesus serving as our Spiritual Atonement, we have become lax, leading to our Spiritual Downfall. Why? We fall upon grace and mercy to save and perfect us as we sit on our hands doing nothing or twiddling our thumbs, wanting others to do what we are unwilling to do for ourselves. As a result, our Spiritual Capacity fails to release the vital information associated with our Divine Destiny.

What is the big deal? Grace and mercy can only take us so far, primarily when they are designed to cover us as we progress toward our Divine Purpose, not to wallow in mediocrity. Meanwhile, the animal kingdom is still intact, doing what it was designed to do. What is that? Finetuning their skills, even if we think they are not.

According to the Heavenly of Heavens, we must focus on moving in the Spirit of Excellence without the pompousness of the Spirit of Perfection.

As we *Storm The Brain*, we must remember that we are all a work-in-progress; therefore, we need to move or take action, *As It Pleases God*. Why? It helps us with our teachability status in or out of the Kingdom. What does this mean? If we are horrible with our people skills, naturally or when dealing with ourselves or others, the same will apply to our Spiritual Skills, causing us to play pretend or mask ourselves.

Focusing on progress rather than perfection allows us to continually improve, self-correct, apologize, and learn from our mistakes. Why? In the Eye of God, perfection is an unattainable goal. In addition, it leads to feelings of inadequacy, self-righteousness, lies, deception, manipulation, and disappointment.

When *Storming The Brain*, we need flexibility and adaptability to help us with challenges, distortions, and unexpected obstacles. For the record, no one is exempt from the natural processes of life. The Cycles and Vicissitudes will come and go, so we must proactively prepare.

When we think we are exempt or perfect, life will test us to see what we are made of. For this reason, it is best to develop a work-in-progress mentality with a willingness to Spiritually Till our own ground without passing the buck or playing the blame game.

Above all, we must believe in ourselves, our potential, and our Divine Blueprint. It provides a Spiritual Covering, illuminating the way to our Divine Purpose. Unbeknown to most, life is designed to serve us, and if we are not in Purpose on purpose, we will find ourselves serving life with a quick fix without healing. How do we gain clarity on our Divine Purpose? It is detailed in the books entitled *Build Your Own Table* and *The WHY Blueprint*.

Storming The Brain regarding our potential is one of the best things we can do for ourselves. There are hidden or untapped potentials that need unveiling, which are usually the foundation of our Predestined Blueprint. Without delegation, we must decide if it will become weak or strong, cracked or solid, leveled or unleveled, and so on. Galatians 6:5 says, *"For each one shall bear his own load."*

Without believing in your potential, you will limit yourself, miss all the incredible opportunities hidden in plain sight, and miss out on how to *Storm Your Brain*.

Complete the chart below to become a work-in-progress, *As It Pleases God*.

STORM YOUR BRAIN
Work-In-Progress

WHAT TO WORK ON **WHY AND HOW?**

BRAINSTORM 13
Set Boundaries

If you do not believe in yourself, who will? If you do not believe in your potential, who will? If you do not set boundaries, who will establish them for you? Who will protect your Spiritual Gifts, Calling, Talents, and Creativity if you do not know what they are?

When *Storming The Brain*, we must set boundaries, period. Why? Distractions are designed to do what it does. What is that? Break us down. Really? Yes, really! Proverbs 25:28 says, *"Whoever has no rule over his own spirit is like a city broken down, without walls."*

We must learn to say 'no' and mean it without being mean, cruel, hateful, or naive. Here is the deal: In the Eye of God, we must know this: " *'The first man Adam became a living being.' The last Adam became a life-giving spirit."* 1 Corinthians 15:45. What does this mean? *"The first man was of the earth, made of dust; the second Man is the Lord from heaven. As was the man of dust, so also are those who are made of dust; and as is the heavenly Man, so also are those who are heavenly. And as we have borne the image of the man of dust, we shall also bear the image of the heavenly Man. Now this I say, brethren, that flesh and blood cannot inherit the kingdom of God; nor does corruption inherit incorruption."* 1 Corinthians 15:47-50.

We must do our due diligence in protecting our Spirit Man from corruption as much as possible. Here is a Biblical tip: *"But let your 'Yes' be 'Yes,' and your 'No,' 'No.' For whatever is more than these is from the evil one."* Matthew 5:37. Here are a few additional tips on effectively setting boundaries, but not limited to such:

- ☐ Involve the Holy Trinity in your equational efforts.
- ☐ Identify your needs, wants, desires, and values.
- ☐ Be clear and direct to avoid misunderstandings.
- ☐ Be specific and straightforward, leaving no room for assumptions.
- ☐ Avoid being passive-aggressive or vague, and set clear expectations for yourself.
- ☐ Exude respect without aggression or being confrontational.
- ☐ Use 'I' statements to avoid blaming, accusing, or pointing the finger. For example, say, 'I assume responsibility for my role in this situation,' instead of saying, 'You are at fault for my situation,' 'You caused this,' or 'You are the problem.'
- ☐ Use 'I' statements to express how their behavior affects you. For example, say, 'I feel overwhelmed when you ask me to do too much' instead of 'You are too needy,' 'You beg too much,' or 'You ask for too much.'
- ☐ Be consistent, stand your ground, and stick to it.
- ☐ Avoid resentment, hatefulness, or unforgiveness.
- ☐ Avoid making lame excuses, spreading lies, or arguing.
- ☐ Stick to the facts, effectively communicating and conveying the Fruits of the Spirit with a smile.
- ☐ Behave Christlike without slandering.

Remember, setting boundaries is not selfish; it reduces stress, anxiety, confusion, fear, and worry, increasing our self-esteem, self-respect, and self-control. Why is this important? The Bible says, *"Keep your heart with all diligence, for out of it spring the issues of life."* Proverbs 4:23.

Setting boundaries can prevent us from being exploited, misused, manipulated, abused, or mistreated. However, 1 Thessalonians 4:11 says, *"That you also aspire to lead a quiet life, to mind your own business, and to work with your own hands, as we commanded you."*

Without assertively minding our own business, we may find ourselves constantly compromising or sacrificing for the sake of others. Why? When we do not focus on living our lives authentically and with dignity, *As It Pleases God*, only to please ourselves, it can have negative repercussions, causing us to whitewash instead of *Storming The Brain*. The chart below is used to begin setting boundaries.

WHERE TO SET BOUNDARIES?

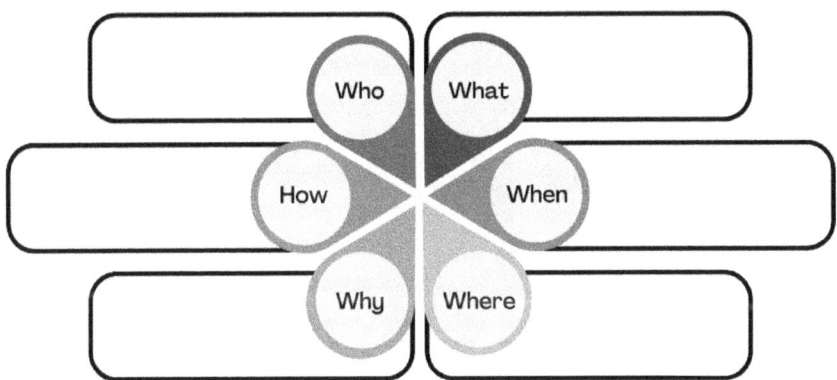

STORM YOUR BRAIN
Boundaries List

- [ ] Where To Set Boundaries?
- [ ] Where To Set Boundaries?
- [ ] Where To Set Boundaries?
- [ ] Where To Set Boundaries?
- [ ] Where To Set Boundaries?
- [ ] Where To Set Boundaries?
- [ ] Where To Set Boundaries?
- [ ] Where To Set Boundaries?
- [ ] Where To Set Boundaries?
- [ ] Where To Set Boundaries?
- [ ] Where To Set Boundaries?
- [ ] Where To Set Boundaries?
- [ ] Where To Set Boundaries?
- [ ] Where To Set Boundaries?
- [ ] Where To Set Boundaries?
- [ ] Where To Set Boundaries?

BRAINSTORM 14
Connect With Nature

How do you feel when you are out in nature? Do you enjoy being outside? What aspects of nature do you find most inspiring? What do you consider to be your favorite outdoor activity? How do you incorporate nature into your daily routine? How do you make time for nature in your busy schedule? What are some of the benefits of spending time in nature? How do you encourage others to connect with nature? Do you know? Do you even care?

According to the Heavenly of Heavens, we must incorporate nature to create an overflow of what is Divine. Why? The Word of God says, "*For by Him all things were created that are in heaven and that are on earth, visible and invisible, whether thrones or dominions or principalities or powers. All things were created through Him and for Him.*" Colossians 1:16.

When *Storming The Brain*, our minds are designed to open up to nature. Why? We are ONE, even if we think we are not or above nature. Remember that we have a nature called human nature...do we think for a minute that it was not derived from nature itself?

Here is what we overlook, "*Then God said, 'Let Us make man in Our image, according to Our likeness; let them have dominion over the fish of the sea, over the birds of the air, and over the cattle, over all the earth and over every creeping thing that creeps on the earth.*' " Genesis 1:26. Where there is dominion, there is always a connection. From Genesis to Revelation, this Spiritual Principle has not changed; we have!

Although nature's elements and benefits nourish us, we sometimes forget to connect to them Mentally, Physically, Emotionally, or Spiritually. Then again, we may think we do not need to connect due to our upgraded lifestyles, but I beg to differ. Meanwhile, when *Storming The Brain*, we will experience more of a release in nature than behind four walls without a picturesque view. What does this mean? Whether in nature or viewing it through the lenses of another, our mind does not know the difference. Therefore, when inside the house, we can provide views of nature, and the mind will respond the same.

For example, when working or inside the house, if we find a way to create a natural environment through pictures or videos, it will soothe the psyche. I like watching WildEarth's live safaris, which allows me to *Storm My Brain* and effectively write how I do. In my *Spirit to Spirit* alone time or during my Divine Downloads, God has allowed nature to teach me valuable Spiritual Principles that man could never teach.

Why must we connect to nature, especially when living our best lives? Fortunately, this is how we were created, and living our best lives is a matter of opinion. Here is what we must know about how we were created: *"And the LORD God formed man of the dust of the ground, and breathed into his nostrils the breath of life; and man became a living being."* Genesis 2:7.

We are SEASONAL Beings. It is a part of our DNA, so God deals with us in Seasons, Cycles, and Vicissitudes with seeds, roots, trees, and fruits. Even if we deny these factors, it does not mean they do not exist. *"To everything, there is a season, A time for every purpose under heaven."* Ecclesiastes 3:1. *"While the earth remains, seedtime and harvest, cold and heat, winter and summer, and day and night shall not cease."* Genesis 8:22.

If we dare to Spiritually Align ourselves with nature, it will naturally soothe the psyche. We are derived from the elements of the earth; therefore, if we respect and connect to nature, *As It Pleases God*, it will give back to us.

How can we make nature make sense? According to the Heavenly of Heavens, connecting to nature's smells, sounds, and fresh air will cause one to relax naturally, reducing stress, hormonal imbalances, or blood pressure. It can also improve cognitive functions, clarity, creativity, composition, and immunity.

Regardless of where we are, who we are, and why we are, we cannot ignore the benefits of improving our moods, thoughts, emotions, memory, behaviors, problem-solving skills, and connection to our Divine Blueprint. We need it, and it needs us.

When *Storming The Brain*, it is best to connect to the Creative Force from within by connecting to nature. What if we cannot get outside? Alternative ways are sometimes necessary when we are limited; however, the best thing about God is that He will always provide another way. Here are various ways to connect to nature, but not limited to such:

- ☐ Hang out in the backyard.
- ☐ Go for a hike in a nearby park or nature reserve.
- ☐ Take a camping trip.
- ☐ Spend a few days in the wilderness.
- ☐ Visit a botanical garden.
- ☐ Learn about different plants and trees.
- ☐ Go birdwatching.
- ☐ Take a nature photography class.
- ☐ Capture the beauty of the outdoors.
- ☐ Go fishing.
- ☐ Go to the park or lake.
- ☐ Go rock climbing.
- ☐ Go kayaking to explore nearby lakes, rivers, and streams.
- ☐ Start a garden.
- ☐ Take a meditation class outside.

- ☐ Visit a local farm or orchard.
- ☐ Take a bike ride.
- ☐ Go horseback riding.
- ☐ Take a journey on a scenic trail.
- ☐ Go to a nature reserve.
- ☐ Go stargazing.
- ☐ Take a nature journaling class.
- ☐ Record your observations, thoughts, or animals.
- ☐ Take a physical or virtual safari. You can experience a virtual LIVE safari with WildEarth on YouTube.
- ☐ Attend a nature-inspired workshop.
- ☐ Do an outside treasure hunt activity.
- ☐ Go on a nature walk.
- ☐ Practice forest or animal therapy.
- ☐ Set up a nature-inspired picnic.
- ☐ Visit a nearby waterfall.
- ☐ Visit natural landmarks.
- ☐ Take a road trip.

Nature provides a peaceful, calming environment to help us feel more relaxed and rejuvenated. It also allows us to disconnect from technology to focus on the present moment, which can improve our *Storming The Brain* experiences.

Please complete the Connecting to Nature Chart, determining the best ways to *Storm Your Brain* and invoke your Creative Genius.

STORM YOUR BRAIN
Connecting to Nature List

- [ ] How To Connect To Nature?
- [ ] How To Connect To Nature?
- [ ] How To Connect To Nature?
- [ ] How To Connect To Nature?
- [ ] How To Connect To Nature?
- [ ] How To Connect To Nature?
- [ ] How To Connect To Nature?
- [ ] How To Connect To Nature?
- [ ] How To Connect To Nature?
- [ ] How To Connect To Nature?
- [ ] How To Connect To Nature?
- [ ] How To Connect To Nature?
- [ ] How To Connect To Nature?
- [ ] How To Connect To Nature?
- [ ] How To Connect To Nature?
- [ ] How To Connect To Nature?
- [ ] How To Connect To Nature?

BRAINSTORM 15
Creative Genius

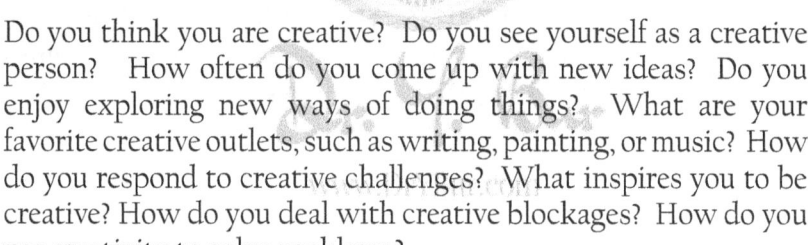

Do you think you are creative? Do you see yourself as a creative person? How often do you come up with new ideas? Do you enjoy exploring new ways of doing things? What are your favorite creative outlets, such as writing, painting, or music? How do you respond to creative challenges? What inspires you to be creative? How do you deal with creative blockages? How do you use creativity to solve problems?

When dealing with our Creative Genius, we must become experts at asking questions and obtaining answers. Invoking our *Creative Genius* will be difficult if we do not like being questioned, fumbling with answers, or being a pathological liar. Why? We will have qualms with authenticity, doing anything to keep up an image to feed our ego, and be willing to destroy anyone who gets in our way. For this reason, our Creative Genius must lie dormant, limiting our ability to *Storm The Brain* the way God intended.

Here is a chart to determine what is blocking your Creative Genius.

WHAT IS BLOCKING YOUR CREATIVE GENIUS

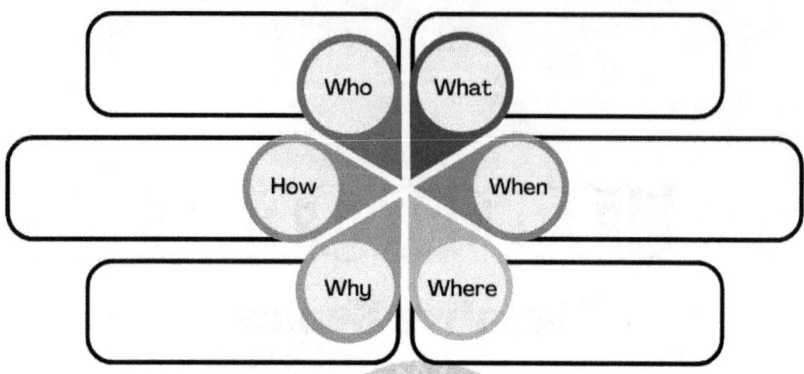

Remember, we are all creative; however, our creativity begins with our MINDSET. Meanwhile, Divine Creativity or our Creative Genius needs a BLUEPRINT. What does this mean in layman's terms? A creative mindset releases the Creative Genius from within once it aligns with our Predestined Blueprint, *As It Pleases God*.

Why do we need to *Storm The Brain* when becoming creative? If we do not initiate the release, it will not violate our free will! For this reason, Romans 12:2 says, *"And do not be conformed to this world, but be transformed by the renewing of your mind, that you may prove what is that good and acceptable and perfect will of God."*

On the other hand, by initiating a *Storm The Brain* session with ourselves, we will get a drizzle of information to release. Why would we get a drizzle? To determine our capacity, or whether we will use it positively or negatively, before a downpouring of what we already possess can occur. Unfortunately, if we cannot handle the drizzle, use it negatively, or the condition is not conducive, *Storming The Brain* must withhold the downpour of our *Creative Genius* until we are ready.

Is our *Creative Genius* real? Absolutely! I am not just writing about this to be writing; I live with the ability to *Storm My Brain* or invoke my *Creative Genius* at the drop of a dime! Nevertheless, *The*

WHY Blueprint aims to prepare willing vessels to *Build Their Own Table* properly and *Storm Their Brain*, getting the information needed to facilitate their Predestined Blueprint.

Whether our Predestined Blueprint is linked through art, music, writing, sports, or any other form of creative expression, we can communicate our thoughts, emotions, desires, and perspectives in ways that can resonate with others by painting mental pictures.

A creative mindset helps develop our problem-solving, querying, and developmental skills to leave no stone unturned, getting us to think inside, outside, around, through, over, and under the box. When we approach our challenges, situations, circumstances, events, and people with a creative mindset, we can come up with innovative ideas, perspectives, and solutions that we might not have considered otherwise. When *Storming The Brain*, we want to remove the self-imposed limitations, bringing forth our Creative Genius. Here are a few tips on how to become a Creative Genius while *Storming The Brain*, but not limited to such:

- ☐ Document everything or keep a journal.
- ☐ Master the ability to ask fact-finding questions in the formation of who, what, when, where, how, and why.
- ☐ Keep an open mind to receiving answers.
- ☐ Be practical and wise without exhibiting foolery.
- ☐ Explore new ideas, concepts, and perspectives.
- ☐ Practice bouncing around ideas with others regularly.
- ☐ Seek out inspiration Mentally, Physically, Emotionally, Spiritually, and Financially.
- ☐ Do not be afraid to take risks.
- ☐ Challenge your assumptions with facts.
- ☐ Seek out new and diverse perspectives and feedback.
- ☐ Engage in activities that positively stimulate your senses or spark your imagination.
- ☐ Create a conducive environment for creativity.
- ☐ Read and remain relevant.

☐ Break down larger projects into smaller, manageable tasks.

Can this really help us? Absolutely. According to the Heavenly of Heavens, *Creative Geniuses* are nurtured, trained, and developed to Spiritually Align with their Blueprinted Purpose.

What if we are a genius without being in purpose? I am not here to discount anyone's abilities or titles. However, a genius in our eyes or man's is not the same as a Creative Genius in the Eye of God. Why? He wants us to complete our Divine Missions, not to create our own, proclaiming titles we have not Spiritually Tilled our own ground for. What is the big deal? When we are not in Purpose on purpose, knowing nothing about our reason for being, it comes with internal voids, emptiness, and insecurities instead of having joy, peace, and serenity. Even if we have become a master at masking our internal qualms, it does not negate why they exist.

Here is what we must understand about the underlying principle hidden within invoking our *Creative Genius* when *Storming Your Brain*: "*Because of these things the wrath of God is coming upon the sons of disobedience, in which you yourselves once walked when you lived in them. But now you yourselves are to put off all these: anger, wrath, malice, blasphemy, filthy language out of your mouth. Do not lie to one another, since you have put off the old man with his deeds, and have put on the new man who is renewed in knowledge according to the image of Him who created him, where there is neither Greek nor Jew, circumcised nor uncircumcised, barbarian, Scythian, slave nor free, but Christ is all and in all.*" Colossians 3:8-11.

Regardless of where and who we are, we are all entitled to the Blood of Jesus, the Holy Spirit, and our *Creative Genius* because we all have a little shade somewhere or with someone. By leaving judgment out of our equational efforts, we will receive more information from the Heavenly of Heavens than we would from judging others. Really? Yes, really! "*Judge not, that you be not judged.*

For with what judgment you judge, you will be judged; and with the measure you use, it will be measured back to you." Matthew 7:1-2.

Increased Creativity

Storming The Brain gets our creative juices flowing from within and with others. We encourage free-flowing, idealistic thoughts, opinions, and associations, allowing ideas to flow freely without judgment or evaluation. However, it is imperative to lock in on the win-win instead of the cynical lose-lose. What makes this so important when increasing our capacity? The win-win mindset expands your capacity, whereas the lose-lose mindset restricts and binds. Even if you are dealing with the appearance of losing, the WIN is hidden amid whatever or whomever.

Stimulating creative thinking leads to unexpected insights, especially in this ability and agility process. Another strategy is to approach the problem from different perspectives. The approach can involve looking at the issue from the perspective of multiple or mirrored views, diverse participants, opposing forces, and so on. Just keep it positive and non-problematic, or without causing harm. For example, for a cop to catch a criminal, he must think like a criminal to outsmart or catch them for the greater good or prevent further harm to the innocent. If not, a cop will 'get got' by the brainstorming of criminality, looking like boo boo the fool for not doing his homework. When it comes down to thinking proactively, they are held to a higher standard, and so are you. Please complete the chart below if you do not know where you are creative.

STORM YOUR BRAIN
Creative Genius List

- [ ] Where Am I Creative?
- [ ] Where Am I Creative?
- [ ] Where Am I Creative?
- [ ] Where Am I Creative?
- [ ] Where Am I Creative?
- [ ] Where Am I Creative?
- [ ] Where Am I Creative?
- [ ] Where Am I Creative?
- [ ] Where Am I Creative?
- [ ] Where Am I Creative?
- [ ] Where Am I Creative?
- [ ] Where Am I Creative?
- [ ] Where Am I Creative?
- [ ] Where Am I Creative?
- [ ] Where Am I Creative?
- [ ] Where Am I Creative?

BRAINSTORM 16
Sense Of Humor

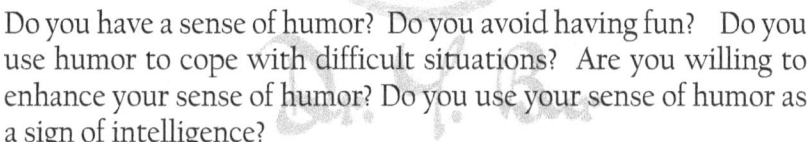

Do you have a sense of humor? Do you avoid having fun? Do you use humor to cope with difficult situations? Are you willing to enhance your sense of humor? Do you use your sense of humor as a sign of intelligence?

Having a sense of humor is not about making foul jokes, being disrespectful, or making fun of people, but about having a cheerful, optimistic, and joyful outlook. Why is this so important? Humor and laughter are powerful Spiritual Tools that promote inner calmness, Mentally, Physically, Emotionally, and Spiritually. We must determine the appropriate time. Why? It can become repulsive or offensive if done at the wrong time or season. According to the Bible, there is "*A time to weep, And a time to laugh; A time to mourn, And a time to dance.*" Ecclesiastes 3:4.

What does our *Sense of Humor* have to do with *Storming The Brain*? We are designed to laugh and smile, even if we do not think they are associated. In the Eye of God, they are interdependently related in releasing Divine Information. To maximize our people skills, God does not want us to be dull or abrasive, nor does He want us to behave foolishly, full of folly and contempt. "*A merry heart does good, like medicine, But a broken spirit dries the bones."* Proverbs 17:22.

God wants us to be diligent, attentive, and receptive to His teachings. If we are uptight, our brain becomes likewise, not absorbing or downloading information as it should. Incorporating playful, fun, or unconventional elements into the *Storming The Brain* process is ideal, promoting stimulative interaction. Doing so may involve using games, puzzles, pictures, comedy, or other activities to stimulate creative thinking.

By approaching problems, solutions, and questions in a playful and lighthearted manner, you can help break down mental barriers and foster a more creative and innovative mindset. Psalm 126:2 says, *"Then our mouth was filled with laughter, And our tongue with singing. Then they said among the nations, 'The Lord has done great things for them.'"* Simply put, our GREAT THINGS could revolve around what brings laughter to the weary soul. Why? Laughter reduces stress, releases tension, and improves our mood. It also strengthens our relationships by creating positive connections with others. Life can be challenging, but humor, peace, and joy can help us navigate difficult times.

Unbeknown to most, God has a sense of humor as well. Really? Yes, really! Most of us think He is rigid and strict, but He is loving, nurturing, understanding, and charismatic, and He has more riddles than the Riddler himself. You will understand what I am discussing once you develop a *Spirit to Spirit* Relationship, *As It Pleases Him*. Nevertheless, until then, here are a few ways to develop your Sense of Humor, but not limited to such:

- ☐ Start by surrounding yourself with people who make you laugh and engage in enjoyable activities.
- ☐ Practice laughing at yourself and not taking things too seriously.
- ☐ Look for the humor in everyday situations and share that laughter with others.
- ☐ Take time to appreciate the simple things in life.
- ☐ Focus on the good or the win-win.

- ☐ Find joy in the little or simple things.
- ☐ Determine to lead a happier, more fulfilling life.
- ☐ Read something funny.
- ☐ Crack funny jokes.

Laughing and experiencing joy can reduce stress and anxiety, lower blood pressure, and boost the immune system. It also improves social connections and strengthens relationships with others.

Having fun can foster collaboration, communication, and problem-solving skills essential for creativity. Really? Yes, really. If we *Storm The Brain* when having fun or when focused, it yields different types of information. Therefore, we want informative and informational perspectives when dealing with *The WHY Blueprint* or *Building Our Own Table*. Why? Once again, we do not want to leave any stone unturned, unchecked, or overlooked.

HUMOR CHART

STORM YOUR BRAIN

STORM YOUR BRAIN
Humor List

- [ ] How To Develop My Humor?
- [ ] How To Develop My Humor?
- [ ] How To Develop My Humor?
- [ ] How To Develop My Humor?
- [ ] How To Develop My Humor?
- [ ] How To Develop My Humor?
- [ ] How To Develop My Humor?
- [ ] How To Develop My Humor?
- [ ] How To Develop My Humor?
- [ ] How To Develop My Humor?
- [ ] How To Develop My Humor?
- [ ] How To Develop My Humor?
- [ ] How To Develop My Humor?
- [ ] How To Develop My Humor?
- [ ] How To Develop My Humor?
- [ ] How To Develop My Humor?

BRAINSTORM 17
Inner Child

Do you connect to your inner child? Do you understand your inner child? Do you silence your inner child? Do you allow your inner child to come out to play? Do you allow your inner child to help you find your passion? Do you allow your inner child to *Storm Your Brain* with you?

We all have an inner child, even if we pretend to be so grown up. What about Corinthians 13:11? It says, *"When I was a child, I spoke as a child, I understood as a child, I thought as a child; but when I became a man, I put away childish things."* It says to put away childish THINGS; it never declares our inner child to be non-existent. Unfortunately, this is how some of us get got by the enemy's tricks of deception, zapping our humility and replacing it with pompousness. So much so that we cannot have fun with our loved ones, causing a relational deficit.

The Bible speaks about bringing childhood foolishness or childishness into adulthood, especially when dealing with people, places, and things. On the other hand, Matthew 18:3 says, *"Assuredly, I say to you, unless you are converted and become as little children, you will by no means enter the Kingdom of Heaven."*

Meanwhile, our inner child has an inner voice that speaks loudly and is still available to help navigate our likes, dislikes, and so on. If we lock our inner child in a box, we will lose our ability to have fun, relate, and effectively communicate. Becoming too serious will put our brains in a gridlock, making us dull, repulsive, and stiff-necked. What does this mean? We cannot see our way clear, our people skills are deplorable, or we lack creativity, while thinking we have it going on.

By tapping into your inner child's carefree and imaginative nature, you can release stress and anxiety, boost your creativity, and find joy in the present moment. It can also help you reconnect with your passions and interests, rediscovering a sense of playfulness that may have been lost in the stresses of adulthood.

So, do not be afraid to let your inner child come out to play occasionally; you might be surprised at how much it can positively impact your life. Above all, neglecting your inner child can lead to feeling stressed, anxious, and disconnected.

When *Storming Your Brain*, you create a win-win situation when you cultivate a sense of adventure and try new experiences. Furthermore, you can open yourself up to personal growth and self-discovery, expand your horizons, and increase your chances of forming new connections and relationships. By stepping out of your comfort zone, you challenge yourself to learn and grow, which can lead to great rewards and experiences.

So take a chance and embrace new challenges; you might find the benefits well worth it. Connect to your *Inner Child* today!

STORM YOUR BRAIN
Inner Child List

- [ ] How To Connect To My Inner Child?
- [ ] How To Connect To My Inner Child?
- [ ] How To Connect To My Inner Child?
- [ ] How To Connect To My Inner Child?
- [ ] How To Connect To My Inner Child?
- [ ] How To Connect To My Inner Child?
- [ ] How To Connect To My Inner Child?
- [ ] How To Connect To My Inner Child?
- [ ] How To Connect To My Inner Child?
- [ ] How To Connect To My Inner Child?
- [ ] How To Connect To My Inner Child?
- [ ] How To Connect To My Inner Child?
- [ ] How To Connect To My Inner Child?
- [ ] How To Connect To My Inner Child?
- [ ] How To Connect To My Inner Child?
- [ ] How To Connect To My Inner Child?

BRAINSTORM 18
Spirit to Spirit

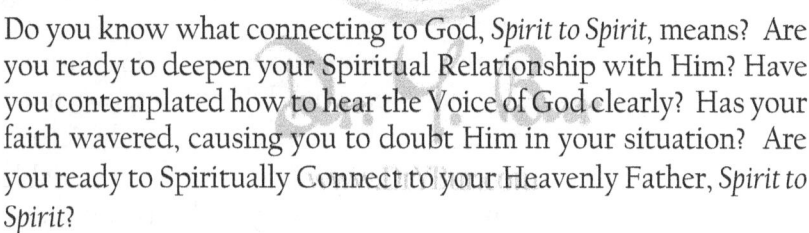

Do you know what connecting to God, *Spirit to Spirit*, means? Are you ready to deepen your Spiritual Relationship with Him? Have you contemplated how to hear the Voice of God clearly? Has your faith wavered, causing you to doubt Him in your situation? Are you ready to Spiritually Connect to your Heavenly Father, *Spirit to Spirit*?

In going deeper, *Spirit to Spirit* to *Storm The Brain*, no one is exempt from fear, doubt, confusion, or any negative character trait. The determining or questionable factors are:

1. What do we do about it (Cast it down, entertain it, or embrace it)?
2. Who do we do it with (God, ourselves, others, or the enemy)?
3. How long do we remain in the condition or mindset with whatever or whomever?

These three factors make the balancing difference in the Eye of God, making us Kingdomly Usable or worldly pliable.

When surrendering to God, our Heavenly Father, *Spirit to Spirit*, we must continually repent and renew our minds. Negativity, unforgiveness, hatefulness, and debauchery will attach themselves to us, opening an old wound derived from the Garden of Eden. For this reason, Ephesians 4:23 tells us how to avoid or solve this problem: "*Be renewed in the spirit of your mind.*"

Developing a *Spirit to Spirit* Relationship with our Heavenly Father is essential to our Spiritual Journey, Predestined Blueprint, and *Storming The Brain*. All of this is based upon Proverbs 3:5-6, "*Trust in the Lord with all your heart, And lean not on your own understanding; In all your ways acknowledge Him, And He shall direct your paths.*" For Him to direct our paths, we must TRUST and ACKNOWLEDGE Him while getting out of our own way.

Of course, we can deepen our relationship with God by taking the time to pray, repent, forgive, read scriptures, meditate, and attend church. However, to learn more about our Divine Purpose or Spiritually Download our Predestined Blueprint, we must engage in a *Spirit to Spirit* Relationship with our Heavenly Father. This *One-on-One* Relationship is designed to create a personable and ongoing process of informative gleaning, understanding, and guidance, requiring patience, commitment, and faith to get to our Divine Status.

With each step we take toward our Heavenly Father, *Spirit to Spirit*, we will feel more connected to Him, experiencing greater Blessings, Favor, and Protection. Can we really experience God's Divine Grace and Mercy in our lives? Absolutely. He does not require perfection; He only asks for willingness, obedience, availability, teachability, understanding, and a work-in-progress mentality.

I have been where you are...although disobedient at times, He never gave up on me. Listen, I was clueless at the beginning of my Spiritual Journey, knowing absolutely nothing at first! I am from the country...the real country, to be exact; therefore, I was not street-smart or savvy, nor was I born with a silver spoon in my mouth, and I was rough around the edges. But God...here again, but God, with the Spiritual Training and charactorial overhaul, *As It Pleased Him*, He did not disappoint.

With Spiritual Pristine, I can relate to everyone on their level, in or out of the Kingdom of God, leaving no WILLING man behind. Therefore, if you follow my lead, *As It Pleases Him*, He will not disappoint you. To deepen your connection with God, *Spirit to Spirit*, and *As It Pleases Him*, you can start by:

- ☐ Committing to Spiritually Till your own ground.
- ☐ Surrendering to God's Divine Will and Ways.
- ☐ Taking the time to pray and commune in your PERSONAL SPACE.
- ☐ Covering yourself with the Blood of Jesus, as your Spiritual Atonement.
- ☐ Ushering in the presence of the Holy Spirit.
- ☐ Repenting, forgiving, and giving thanks.
- ☐ Reading the Bible.
- ☐ Meditating on the Word of God and using positive affirmations.
- ☐ Documenting your *Spirit to Spirit* conversations, instructions, or answers.
- ☐ Using the Fruits of the Spirit (Love, Joy, Peace, Patience, Kindness, Goodness, Faithfulness, Gentleness, and Self-Control).
- ☐ Behaving Christlike, purging all jealousy, envy, pride, greed, coveting, contention, and competitiveness out of your system.

These Spiritual Actions will help you connect with the DIVINE and find peace, comfort, and guidance daily. Remember that building a Spiritual Relationship is a journey, not a destination. With each step you take towards your Heavenly Father, you will feel more connected to Him and experience His Divine Presence. In addition, you can *Storm Your Brain* at the drop of a dime,

Spiritually Downloading from the Heavenly of Heavens. Is this really possible? Absolutely! I would not say it if it were not so.

If I can do it, *As It Pleases God*, you can too! As a matter of fact, this is nothing new; it is ANCIENT. We have simply forgotten about our astounding Spiritual Capabilities and Tools. Besides, when *Storming Your Brain*, the only limits you have are the ones you place upon yourself.

What are the best times to connect *Spirit to Spirit* with our Heavenly Father? The superlative moment to develop a Spiritual Relationship is when you have a quiet and peaceful environment to focus on your Divine Connection with God Almighty. Since we are all different, some people find early morning or late night conducive, while others prefer Spiritually Connecting during their lunch break or in the evening.

Once we engage *Spirit to Spirit*, God will set the tone and time of our Divine Downloads. The most important thing is Spiritually Connecting with Him and consistently deepening our Spiritual Relationship, gleaning the Divine Wisdom, Secrets, Treasures, Favor, and so on.

BRAINSTORM 19
Passionate Purpose

Do you know your passion? Do you know your purpose? Do you know how to develop them both? When *Storming The Brain*, humility is a prerequisite to learning and mastering the differences between our inner passions and Divine Purpose. If you think you know more than your brain does, it will not yield as it should. It will withhold information to make you look like a fool. What is more embarrassing than getting a side-eye from those we beat down with our ego, as they realize we are clueless about our reason for being?

Do we need a *Spirit to Spirit* Relationship to connect to our passion (What we love doing)? Since we all have self-created and God-Given passions, it is not necessary to have a Spiritual Relationship to connect to them because we are creatures of habit and adaptation. Passion or not, we can become good at anything we persist at based upon the Law of Adaptation and Use, our survival instincts, and our animalistic nature.

On the other hand, it DOES limit our portion or capacity to Divinely Connect to them, *As It Pleases God*, as we opt to please ourselves. Simply put, we cannot operate at our full capacity without adding God into our equational efforts. Even if we think we are good, we are better with God Almighty. Really? Yes, really! Therefore, we must learn how to combine or break down our passion and purpose, giving us an idea of what we are presenting to God. If we do not know what we are presenting, then we will not understand or interpret what is DIVINE. Here are a few charts to help *Storm Your Brain* to determine what works from passion to purpose and vice versa.

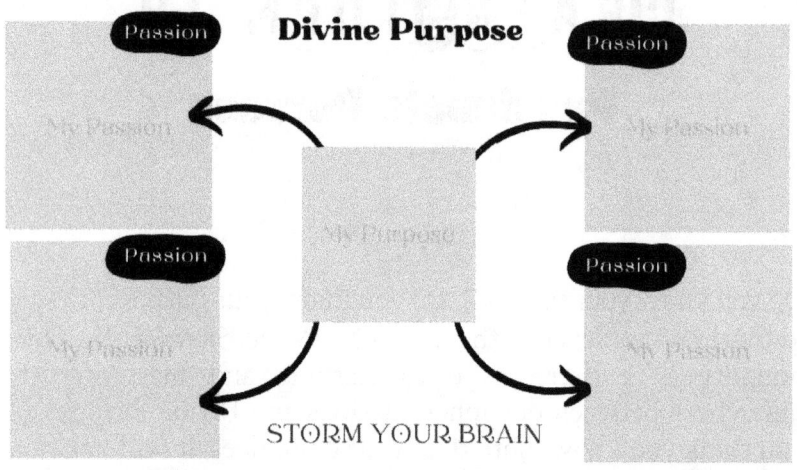

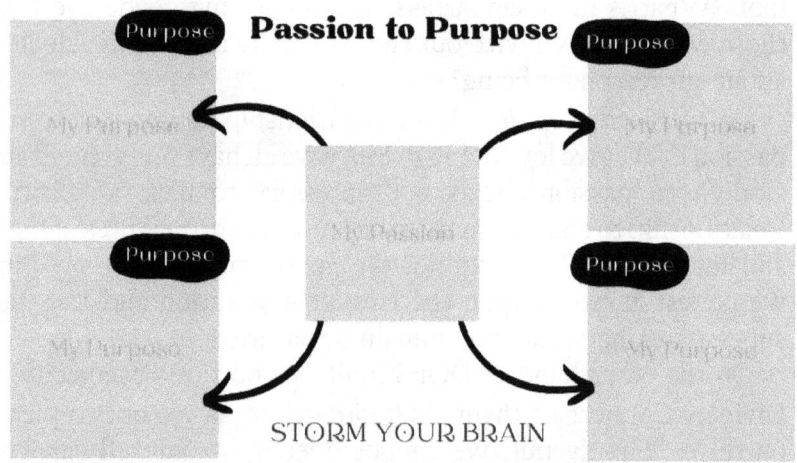

STORM YOUR BRAIN
Purpose List

- [ ] What Is My Purpose For The Greater Good?
- [ ] What Is My Purpose For The Greater Good?
- [ ] What Is My Purpose For The Greater Good?
- [ ] What Is My Purpose For The Greater Good?
- [ ] What Is My Purpose For The Greater Good?
- [ ] What Is My Purpose For The Greater Good?
- [ ] What Is My Purpose For The Greater Good?
- [ ] What Is My Purpose For The Greater Good?
- [ ] What Is My Purpose For The Greater Good?
- [ ] What Is My Purpose For The Greater Good?
- [ ] What Is My Purpose For The Greater Good?
- [ ] What Is My Purpose For The Greater Good?
- [ ] What Is My Purpose For The Greater Good?
- [ ] What Is My Purpose For The Greater Good?
- [ ] What Is My Purpose For The Greater Good?
- [ ] What Is My Purpose For The Greater Good?

STORM YOUR BRAIN
Passion List

- [ ] What Is My Passion?
- [ ] What Is My Passion?
- [ ] What Is My Passion?
- [ ] What Is My Passion?
- [ ] What Is My Passion?
- [ ] What Is My Passion?
- [ ] What Is My Passion?
- [ ] What Is My Passion?
- [ ] What Is My Passion?
- [ ] What Is My Passion?
- [ ] What Is My Passion?
- [ ] What Is My Passion?
- [ ] What Is My Passion?
- [ ] What Is My Passion?
- [ ] What Is My Passion?
- [ ] What Is My Passion?

It is okay to redo your charts until you get them right. I had to redo, revamp, regraft, and restructure so many times that I lost count, but I did not give up, and nor should you...Keep it moving in the Spirit of Excellence. In the interim, not connecting to our passion or purpose, *As It Pleases God*, interferes with our level of peace.

Additionally, when embarking on our *Passionate Purpose*, practicing peace-loving humility can help us avoid arrogance and entitlement, which can be detrimental to our personal growth, success, and people skills.

One way to operate in our *Passionate Purpose* with peace-loving humility is to acknowledge a few things, but not limited to such:

- ☐ We are not perfect.
- ☐ We have room for improvement and growth.
- ☐ We possess a work-in-progress mentality.
- ☐ We are willing to listen, learn, and understand.
- ☐ We are open to considering other perspectives, even if we disagree.
- ☐ We should also recognize and appreciate the contributions of others.
- ☐ We are not seeking to take credit for everything ourselves.
- ☐ We are open-minded.
- ☐ We are willing to learn from our mistakes and failures.
- ☐ We are willing to have and build stronger relationships with God, ourselves, and others.

Using this list can help us communicate effectively and build trust and respect with God, ourselves, and others, allowing us to *Storm The Brain* with an openness to receive. In addition, it can foster a collaborative and supportive environment, in or out of our Spiritual Classroom. By recognizing and acknowledging our limitations, we can become more empathetic and understanding towards others, and ultimately improve our relationships with them, gleaning wisdom on high, especially when we can acknowledge when we are wrong or have made a mistake without having to whitewash or hide.

BRAINSTORM 20

Peace, Be Still

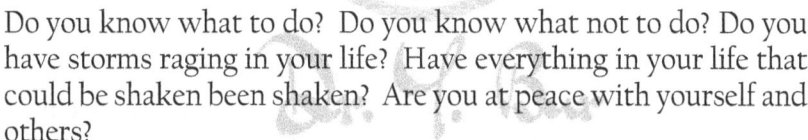

Do you know what to do? Do you know what not to do? Do you have storms raging in your life? Have everything in your life that could be shaken been shaken? Are you at peace with yourself and others?

We often think of storms as harmful, destructive, or intrusive; however, on behalf of our Predestined Blueprint, it is profoundly designed for our good. How so? For example, when drinking a non-carbonated beverage, would you gulp it down before shaking it? Or would you shake it before drinking it? Of course, we would shake it before consuming it to maximize its highest and best-flavored use. We are no different in the Eye of God.

If someone is crying Holy, Holy, Holy, and they have never been shaken to the core, I do not believe them. With all due respect, if they have not experienced the Vicissitudes and Cycles of Life, I do not believe them. If they do not exhibit any of the Fruits of the Spirit, I do not believe them. If they have zero control over their tongue, I do not believe them. If they are trying to convince me about their Holy Status, I do not believe them. Why? Storms are designed to see what we are made of. If we have not been tested, *As It Pleases God*, the HOLE in them still exists.

How can I say such a thing? I am not here to throw the rock and hide my hands but to speak the truth in love, pointing them in the correct direction. For example, but not limited to such:

- ☐ Without power, money, and sex, I want to see what they would do.
- ☐ Without a job, I want to see what they would do.
- ☐ Without support or love, I want to see what they would do.
- ☐ I want to see what they would do when rejected, ostracized, and thrown under the bus.
- ☐ I want to see what they would do when treated like junkyard dogs.
- ☐ I want to see what they would do when no one is watching.

The bottom line is that if we want to see what our brains are made of, we must STORM it. Why? If we can make it *Be Still*, we have something to work with. On the other hand, if it goes haywire, then we have more work to do.

When *Storming The Brain*, it is only fair to parallel this after Jesus and His disciples in a boat when a great windstorm arose in Mark 4:35-41. The waves violently beat against the boat, filling it with water and causing the disciples to become afraid. Jesus, asleep on a pillow, was awakened by His disciples and rebuked the wind, saying, 'Peace, be still!' The wind then ceased, and there was a great calm. Jesus then asked His disciples why they were so fearful and had no faith.

Regardless of where we are or what is happening around us, we have the Spiritual Right from the Heavenly of Heavens to *Storm The Brain*, and demand peace. Just as Jesus calmed the storm with His words, we can calm the storms in our lives with words as well. How? By *Storming The Brain*! For example, but not limited to such:

- ☐ When chaos and danger are threatening us, *Storm The Brain*.
- ☐ When we encounter Mental, Physical, Emotional, and Spiritual woes, *Storm The Brain*.
- ☐ When our faith is shaken, *Storm The Brain*.
- ☐ When our endurance is being tested, *Storm The Brain*.
- ☐ When we feel helpless, hopeless, or doubtful, *Storm The Brain*.
- ☐ When we need Divine Intervention, *Storm The Brain*.
- ☐ When our soul is crying out, *Storm The Brain*.
- ☐ When we feel abandoned, *Storm The Brain*.
- ☐ When we do not know who to trust, *Storm The Brain*.
- ☐ When we are worried, *Storm The Brain*.
- ☐ When we are losing control of ourselves, *Storm The Brain*.
- ☐ When we have a mission to accomplish, *Storm The Brain*.
- ☐ When rebellion or disobedience is rising against us, *Storm The Brain*.
- ☐ When we need a miracle, *Storm The Brain*.
- ☐ When we want to understand our Divine Blueprint, *Storm The Brain*.

We often become so focused on our next step that we forget about being at peace. Nevertheless, when *Storming The Brain*, whether in the know or not, we must be at peace with ourselves and others. Why? We must remain grounded to avoid becoming unhinged or prematurely unrooted.

When we are humble, we are more willing to listen to God, ourselves, and others while considering and respecting different perspectives. And, being that we are not a one-pony rodeo, we need people, and they need us. Here are a few ways we lose or disrupt our peace while doing what we love:

- When what we are doing is NOT connected to our Divine Passion or Blueprint, we forfeit our peace.
- When our self-made passion or purpose is not currently being used or hidden under a rock, we forfeit our peace.
- When we engage in debauchery, we forfeit our peace.
- When we willfully indulge in rebellion, disobedience, deceit, dullness, or having a stiff neck toward God, we will forfeit our peace.
- When we instigate confusion, chaos, bullying, or manipulation, we forfeit our peace.
- When we have loose lips or an untamed tongue, we forfeit our peace.
- When we allow the mind to run wild with negative thoughts, beliefs, and desires, we forfeit our peace.
- When we allow our rotten fruits to remain uncorrected, willingly spoiling the fruits of another, we forfeit our peace.
- When we think we are above God Almighty, we forfeit our peace.
- When we intentionally devise debaucherous plans, causing the downfall of the innocent, we forfeit our peace.
- When we pride ourselves on lying to others to deceive, manipulate, and use them, we forfeit our peace.

What if we do not lose our peace when engaging in these activities? It means our conscience is keeled or our Spiritual Compass is warped. What does this mean? If we do not feel the lack of peace, we are covering it up with something else associated with the lust of the eyes, the lusts of the flesh, and the pride of life. Plus, the mind will become consumed with power, money, and sex, feeding our habits, vices, and longings, affecting our *Spirit to Spirit* Relations.

On the other hand, when doing what we love, we may NOT experience our soulish longing from within the psyche. Yet, the moment we stop doing what we do, the voided hole returns as a vice grip, yoking us again, looking for another fix. Therefore, it is always best to add our *Spirit to Spirit* Relationship into the equation of all things to experience the Fruits of the Spirit. Why? It keeps us from experiencing our psyche negatively lapsing, treating us like a yo-yo, or placing us in a cycle of déjà vu.

In our *Spirit to Spirit* Relations, the goal is to give God what He wants, and He will give us what we desire. Really? Yes, really! As long as it is good for us and aligns with our Divine Blueprint, He will not withhold any good thing. Is this Biblical? I would have it no other way: Psalm 84:11 says, "*For the Lord God is a sun and shield; the Lord will give grace and glory; no good thing will He withhold from those who walk uprightly.*" To walk uprightly in our *Passionate Purpose*, you must know two things:

1. What Brings Inner Peace To Your Soul?
2. What Disrupts Your Peace?

Before moving to the charts, know this: "*Trust in the LORD, and do good; Dwell in the land, and feed on His faithfulness. Delight yourself also in the LORD, And He shall give you the desires of your heart. Commit your way to the LORD, Trust also in Him, And He shall bring it to pass. He shall bring forth your righteousness as the light, And your justice as the noonday. Rest in the LORD, and wait patiently for Him; Do not fret because of him who prospers in his way, Because of the man who brings wicked schemes to pass.*" Psalm 37:3-7.

STORM YOUR BRAIN
Peace List

- [ ] What Brings Inner Peace To Your Soul?
- [ ] What Brings Inner Peace To Your Soul?
- [ ] What Brings Inner Peace To Your Soul?
- [ ] What Brings Inner Peace To Your Soul?
- [ ] What Brings Inner Peace To Your Soul?
- [ ] What Brings Inner Peace To Your Soul?
- [ ] What Brings Inner Peace To Your Soul?
- [ ] What Brings Inner Peace To Your Soul?
- [ ] What Brings Inner Peace To Your Soul?
- [ ] What Brings Inner Peace To Your Soul?
- [ ] What Brings Inner Peace To Your Soul?
- [ ] What Brings Inner Peace To Your Soul?
- [ ] What Brings Inner Peace To Your Soul?
- [ ] What Brings Inner Peace To Your Soul?
- [ ] What Brings Inner Peace To Your Soul?
- [ ] What Brings Inner Peace To Your Soul?

STORM YOUR BRAIN
Peace Disruption List

- [ ] What Disrupts Your Peace?
- [ ] What Disrupts Your Peace?
- [ ] What Disrupts Your Peace?
- [ ] What Disrupts Your Peace?
- [ ] What Disrupts Your Peace?
- [ ] What Disrupts Your Peace?
- [ ] What Disrupts Your Peace?
- [ ] What Disrupts Your Peace?
- [ ] What Disrupts Your Peace?
- [ ] What Disrupts Your Peace?
- [ ] What Disrupts Your Peace?
- [ ] What Disrupts Your Peace?
- [ ] What Disrupts Your Peace?
- [ ] What Disrupts Your Peace?
- [ ] What Disrupts Your Peace?
- [ ] What Disrupts Your Peace?

BRAINSTORM 21

Storm Your Brain

Storming Your Brain is a creative process to generate ideas, thoughts, and solutions to a problem, create an event, develop tasks, orchestrate directions, and so on. When doing so, no limit is set to prevent you from *Storming Your Brain* the way you desire. Why? It should remain free to choose good or bad, right or wrong, positive or negative, and so on. Sometimes, you must understand the bad to get to the good, the wrong to get to the right, and the negative to get to the positive. In *The WHY Blueprint*, this is called Reverse Engineering.

Storming The Brain is a valuable tool for anyone, especially writers, designers, singers, business leaders, entrepreneurs, or anyone needing fresh, new, or reformed ideas, but not limited to such.

Nevertheless, when *Storming The Brain*, you must know what you are trying to achieve. Please write down the problem or task you are trying to solve so you can keep it in mind as you generate ideas. Here is the chart to help you in this process.

STORM YOUR BRAIN

GOALS

GOAL:

- WHAT
- WHY
- WHERE
- WHEN
- HOW
- WITH WHOM

When *Storming The Brain*, it is imperative to establish a secure setting. When the brain is geared to produce, *As It Pleases God*, we must respect it enough to prepare to receive. For example, we would never walk into a restaurant as paying customers to eat dinner without tables to sit at, plates to eat from, silverware to eat with, cups to drink from, pots to cook the food, or food to serve us. The same applies to Divine Information; we must prepare the table for it. Even if we do not get anything, PREPARE IT!

For example, when the Canaanite woman came to Jesus asking for help and healing for her daughter. *"And she said, 'Yes, Lord, yet even the little dogs eat the crumbs which fall from their masters' table.' "* Matthew 15:27. She came prepared to receive, and so should we. Really? Yes, really! Her results were listed in Matthew 15:28: *"Then Jesus answered and said to her, 'O woman, great is your faith! Let it be to you as you desire.' And her daughter was healed from that very hour."*

Storming Your Brain can deliver, heal, protect, propel, or do whatever you need if you allow it to do so, as long as it Spiritually Aligns with your Predestined Blueprint. Here is a sample table:

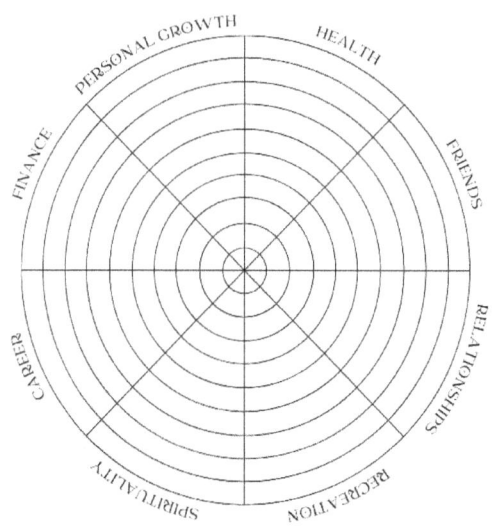

STORM YOUR BRAIN

PREPARE YOUR TABLE

What Are You Preparing For?

Item	What Is The First Thing That Comes To Mind?
Item	What Is The First Thing That Comes To Mind?
Item	What Is The First Thing That Comes To Mind?
Item	What Is The First Thing That Comes To Mind?
Item	What Is The First Thing That Comes To Mind?
Item	What Is The First Thing That Comes To Mind?
Item	What Is The First Thing That Comes To Mind?
Item	What Is The First Thing That Comes To Mind?
Item	What Is The First Thing That Comes To Mind?
Item	What Is The First Thing That Comes To Mind?
Item	What Is The First Thing That Comes To Mind?
Item	What Is The First Thing That Comes To Mind?
Item	What Is The First Thing That Comes To Mind?

The Release

Once we prepare the table for *Storming The Brain*, we must open the Mind, Body, and Soul to squash all negative or debauched feelings, creating a non-judgment zone. Why? It releases the negative grip of emotional or mental baggage, weighing the brain down.

The goal of *Storming The Brain* is to release it to produce, *As It Pleases God*. According to the Heavenly of Heavens, everything we need is already there. We must place a Spiritual Demand on the information needed to facilitate whatever, whenever, however, wherever, why-ever, and with whomever, leaving no stone unturned.

Listed below is the Release Chart; please use it before going any further.

THE RELEASE CHART

Release Chart

STORM YOUR BRAIN

Knowing what to release and why we must let go can change the trajectory of our lives. Therefore, we must become comfortable with who we are and why we are, making our practical our hands-on reality.

Thought Conversions

When your mind is free, it will produce more relevant thoughts, ideas, and concepts, taking you from where you are to your NEXT, *As It Pleases God.* More importantly, when *Storming Your Brain*, do not despise the day of small thoughts, people of small thoughts, or the diamonds in the rough.

When *Storming The Brain*, we must challenge the upgrade. What does this mean? When we have a thought, we have the right to test or challenge it, *As It Pleases God.* By using this Spiritual Law, we can challenge it to produce better. Is this not being ungrateful? Absolutely not!

When downloading information from the Heavenly of Heavens, we deserve the best of the best, nor should we be deceived; therefore, we can TEST the Spirit. Really? Yes, really. Please allow me to Spiritually Align: *"Beloved, do not believe every spirit, but test the spirits, whether they are of God; because many false prophets have gone out into the world."* 1 John 4:1. We often limit this scripture to testing people with mind games and manmade tests. Unfortunately, this is how we become deceived, missing out on what is DIVINE. We have the Spiritual Right to TEST people, places, things, thoughts, emotions, or whatever by its FRUITS.

What do our fruits have to do with *Storming The Brain*? We must incorporate the Fruits of the Spirit if we desire top-notch, quality information, ideas, thoughts, beliefs, or whatever. Why? It removes the law governing the flow. Please allow me to Spiritually Align: *"But the fruit of the Spirit is love, joy, peace, patience, kindness, goodness, faithfulness, gentleness, self-control. Against such, there is no law."* Galatians 5:22-23. The bottom line is that it helps us to realign negative, unfruitful, or debauched thoughts without rejecting the information; therefore, it keeps following with better, stronger, and wiser thoughts, ideas, concepts, and precepts. Here is a chart to help challenge ourselves.

STORM YOUR BRAIN
Thought Conversions

ORIGINAL THOUGHT ⋯➤ **BETTER THOUGHT**

Idea Trigger

Once we *Storm The Brain* to produce better thoughts, we can train the brain to produce *Idea* Triggers. This process should not have anything to do with our negative triggers or trauma; this is why we did the *Release Chart* before getting to this one. If you have not completed the above chart, I suggest you do so to maximize your highest and greatest potential.

This Divine Concept is a way of getting our brain to produce by looking at words, pictures, paintings, mind maps, and so on. Then again, we can also use hearing or action as an Idea Trigger.

Everyone is different; therefore, we must find what works for us. Amid doing so, we must add the Holy Spirit into our equational efforts to download our Divine Potentiality. Blasphemy, right? Wrong. *"But God has revealed them to us through His Spirit. For the Spirit searches all things, yes, the deep things of God. For what man knows the things of a man except the spirit of the man which is in him? Even so no one knows the things of God except the Spirit of God."* 1 Corinthians 2:10-11.

Greatness lies within each of us, making it imperative to learn how to Spiritually Trigger our Divine Greatness to come forth. From the Ancient of Days until now, *Idea Triggering* has been an excellent way to *Storm The Brain*, causing it to produce, *As It Pleases God*. How do I know? The Bible says, *"But as it is written: 'Eye has not seen, nor ear heard, Nor have entered into the heart of man The things which God has prepared for those who love Him.'"* If we have not tapped into what He has for us, it means there is MORE!

Then again, if we settle for less, we have free will to do so. But for me and my house, I want everything that belongs to us without having a tittle fall to the ground. Is this not being greedy? Absolutely not. I want what belongs to us; I am not asking for what belongs to another. I want me and mine, period!

STORM YOUR BRAIN

IDEA TRIGGER
ACTION TRIGGERING

MY GOAL:

STOP DOING

DO LESS OF

KEEP DOING

DO MORE OF

START DOING

IDEA TRIGGER

Build-An-Idea Mentality

To generate ideas, we must document them, right? With a *Build-An-Idea Mentality*, we document to build, one word upon another, one thought upon the next, one whatever upon the next, creating a track record or trail of viable information that can be used now or later.

With our *Build-An-Idea Mentality*, we start by writing down as many ideas as possible without judging or evaluating them. Use a journal, whiteboard, or flip chart to capture all the suggested ideas, or designate someone to document on paper. Why is this so important? *"The heart of the prudent acquires knowledge, And the ear of the wise seeks knowledge."* Proverbs 18:15.

Encouraging the *Build-An-Idea Mentality* helps us gain the Power of God if we approach it correctly. Is this Biblical? Absolutely. *"And my speech and my preaching were not with persuasive words of human wisdom, but in demonstration of the Spirit and of power, that your faith should not be in the wisdom of men but in the power of God."* 1 Corinthians 2:4-5.

We cannot miss a beat when building upon the Word of God with His Divine Power. On the other hand, building without Him, anything goes. What does this mean? We cannot expect God to stand on our word just because we say so.

Nevertheless, if we approach all things with His Divine Word, *As It Pleases Him*, He will do what it takes to make our names GREAT. According to the Bible, *"A man's gift makes room for him, And brings him before great men."* Proverbs 18:16.

What if we do not have a gift? We all have something to work with, even if it does not appear so. For this reason, *Storming The Brain* becomes a valuable Spiritual Tool, helping us map out or pinpoint what we have in our hands. Here are a few tips, but not limited to such:

- ☐ *Storm Your Brain* alone and then with a group.
- ☐ Build on your ideas without help.
- ☐ Build another profile with the help of others.

- ☐ Build a bridge between the two sessions.
- ☐ Build on or expand the results of the previous session.
- ☐ Build a formal repeat session, strengthening your ideas, thoughts, or whatever.
- ☐ Rinse and repeat until your *Build-An-Idea Mentality* becomes a masterpiece.

When *Storming The Brain*, if you dare to take this up a notch to incorporate positive mind-storming, thought-storming, word-storming, action-storming, and character-storming, it will make you uniquely UNSTOPPABLE. Whether doing so alone or with someone else, it is a powerful tool guaranteed to revolutionize your life. Here are the benefits of brainstorming in conjunction with your mind, thoughts, words, actions, and character, but not limited to such:

- ☐ Increased Creativity
- ☐ Improved Communication
- ☐ Enhanced Problem-Solving
- ☐ Increased Motivation
- ☐ Greater Productivity
- ☐ Improved Decision-Making
- ☐ Increased Confidence
- ☐ Greater Sense of Ownership
- ☐ Increased Innovation
- ☐ Improved Problem-Identification
- ☐ Increased Teamwork
- ☐ Enhanced Learning
- ☐ Increased Engagement

STORM YOUR BRAIN

BUILD-AN-IDEA MENTALITY

	IDEAS, THOUGHTS, ACTIONS, AND DESIRES	🕒
01	Build-An-Idea Block 1	
02	Build-An-Idea Block 2	
03	Build-An-Idea Block 3	
04	Build-An-Idea Block 4	
05	Build-An-Idea Block 5	
06	Build-An-Idea Block 6	
07	Build-An-Idea Block 7	
08	Build-An-Idea Block 8	
09	Build-An-Idea Block 9	
10	Build-An-Idea Block 10	

FINAL IDEA

Overcoming Blocks

Do you have writer's block? Do you feel as if your mind is blank? Do you lack ideas? Are your mental cobwebs making it difficult to envision your next move?

According to the Heavenly of Heavens, if we draw a blank or become blocked, the conveyance system is blocked. Therefore, freedom and comfort must be re-established with another TRIGGER word, thought, belief, or a relevant story, building upon the previous. What does this mean? Reset the expectations and reconnect by telling a story with triggered, encouraging, and comforting words of motivation. Here are a few ways to remove mental blockages, but not limited to such:

- ☐ Take a break.
- ☐ Step away from the problem for a few minutes to pray.
- ☐ Refine and evaluate what you are doing.
- ☐ Generate a list of ideas and start evaluating them.
- ☐ Complete an Idea Trigger Chart.
- ☐ Repeat this until the block yields: *"My tongue is the pen of a ready writer."* Psalm 45:1b.

Storming The Brain allows us to think inside, outside, around, through, over, and under the box. It also helps to develop innovative ideas as building blocks to create a whole. When broken down into stages, it helps break down mental barriers and encourages the free flow of ideas without criticism or judgment in multiplicity forms.

This dissecting analogy is similar to fixing a car, where something must be broken down or removed to fix the issue and then put back together to complete the job. The mind is the same way. When *Storming The Brain*, dissection must occur to enhance, repair, or fix someone or something, from the least to the greatest or vice versa. More importantly, no one is exempt from learning in this manner. When someone says, 'They have it all together,' or 'They do not have anything to work on,' I know it is not true.

Deception is one of the greatest downfalls of humanity. For this reason, it is to our advantage to develop a work-in-progress mentality, enabling productive and fruitful growth and overcoming any blockage preventing us from *Doing Business*. Here is a SMART Chart.

STORM YOUR BRAIN

OVERCOMING BLOCKS

SMART CHART

S	**SPECIFIC** — WHAT DO I WANT TO ACCOMPLISH?	
M	**MEASURABLE** — HOW WILL I KNOW WHEN IT IS ACCOMPLISHED?	
A	**ACHIEVABLE** — HOW CAN THE GOAL BE ACCOMPLISHED?	
R	**RELEVANT** — DOES THIS SEEM WORTHWHILE?	
T	**TIME BOUND** — WHEN CAN I ACCOMPLISH THIS GOAL?	

BRAINSTORM 22

Spirit to Business

Are you ready to do business? Are you ready to put your Spiritual Talents, Gifts, Calling, or Creativity to work? Are you wondering how to capitalize on or start a business with your Spiritual Gifts? Are you questioning how to use your Spiritual Gifts to differentiate your business from competitors? Do you know what legal structure you should choose for your business?

Now that you are an expert at *Storming Your Brain*, and possess the Spiritual Tools needed to put pen to paper, it is time to put on my business hat.

1. *The WHY Blueprint* helped you to understand that *What Hurt You is What Heals You*.
2. *Building Your Own Table* assisted in helping you take responsibility and build yourself up with one brick at a time.
3. *Storming Your Brain* facilitates getting what is in your brain formally documented.

Spirit to Spirit, it is time to learn about the *Spirit to Business* Approach, *As It Pleases God*. We must add God into our efforts to do business, using our Spiritual Gifts, Talents, and Creativity.

The *Spirit to Business* Approach is not commonly used in our Business Modules, but I personally think it should be; therefore, let me roll out the red carpet, creating a legacy with this Spiritual Approach, *As It Pleases God*.

What is the *Spirit to Business* Approach? It is setting up a business using what we have in our hands, based upon Jesus' saying, "*Cast the net on the right side of the boat, and you will find some. So they cast, and now they were not able to draw it in because of the multitude of fish.*" John 21:6. In relevant terms of today, operating in the Spirit of Righteousness has more leverage than casting ill will, debauchery, pilfering, and scheming, casting our nets on the wrong side of the boat. Regardless of who we are, why we are, or which side of the boat we choose, we have free will to decide what we desire, whether right or wrong.

For *Storming The Brain*, we must be prepared when casting our nets, *As It Pleases God*. We cannot get ready when the opportunity presents itself; we must be ready! If your charts are not completed, it tells me that you are not ready. Disobedience is an indication of a lack of readiness in the Kingdom. Then again, if you think you are above completing the charts because you have it all together, unfortunately, there may be a Spiritual Disconnect somewhere. I would suggest you reconnect and reapproach, *As It Pleases God*. Why must we reapproach? I am not doing this for me; it is for YOU.

"*So the Lord said to him, 'What is that in your hand?' He said, 'A rod.'* " Exodus 4:2. Whatever you need is in your hands, use it, use them, and use that, leaving no stone unturned until your MULTITUDE becomes your FORTITUDE, *As It Pleases God*.

How do we make multitude and fortitude make sense? What is in your hand (Gift, Calling, Creativity, Talents, or Purpose) has a multiplying ability to produce in multitudes, granting you the power and substance needed to move to the next level of Divine Greatness.

Simply put, if you follow instructions, you will have more than enough Mentally, Physically, Emotionally, Spiritually, and Financially with no shame attached. Then again, by ignoring Divine Instructions, we may operate in a deficit with bouts of shame, issues with self-esteem, or an identity crisis. Is this Biblical? Absolutely!

"Therefore I remind you to stir up the gift of God which is in you through the laying on of my hands. For God has not given us a spirit of fear, but of power and of love and of a sound mind. Therefore do not be ashamed of the testimony of our Lord, nor of me His prisoner, but share with me in the sufferings for the gospel according to the power of God." 2 Timothy 1:6-8. If we are experiencing fear, powerlessness, unlovability, shamefulness, or feeling unsound, we must reevaluate who we receive our instructions from (God, ourselves, others, or the enemy). For this reason, with our *Spirit to Business* Approach, we must *Stay Focused*.

Stay Focused

Before going any further, when Spiritually Tilling our own ground to become Spiritually Great, know this: *"No one, having put his hand to the plow, and looking back, is fit for the kingdom of God."* Luke 9:62. We cannot be wishy-washy going back and forth...one day, we are for the Kingdom, and the next day we are for the world.

When *Storming The Brain* and *Staying Focused*, we must make a vital decision about our *Spirit to Business* Approach. Plus, *"If it seems evil to you to serve the Lord, choose for yourselves this day whom you will serve, whether the gods which your fathers served that were on the other side of the River, or the gods of the Amorites, in whose land you dwell. But as for me and my house, we will serve the Lord."* Joshua 24:15.

When having a *Spirit to Spirit* Relationship with our Heavenly Father and tapping into a *Spirit to Business* Approach, *As It Pleases*

Him, the information we need for our Predestined Blueprint will find us. Remember, everything we need is already there; we must Spiritually Align to place a DEMAND on it. Really? Yes, really! With this ideal relational status, here is the Spiritual Seal we must know and use as Spiritual Leverage: *"Therefore do not fear them. For there is nothing covered that will not be revealed, and hidden that will not be known. 'Whatever I tell you in the dark, speak in the light; and what you hear in the ear, preach on the housetops.'"* Matthew 10:26-27.

More importantly, we do not need to go viral or reach the masses; all we need is one! What does this mean? Do your absolute best with one person or what you have in your hand, and the Law of Reciprocity must YIELD to us. How? If we plant one good seed based upon the Fruits of the Spirit, it must produce!

On the other hand, if we plant multiple seeds badly, we will reap bad harvests, causing more harm than good, and having to play cleanup. For this reason, being a good steward over one careful seed, we can change the trajectory of our lives, especially if God trusts us to feed His sheep. By feeding one sheep well and *Lifting Our Rod, As It Pleases God*, they will bring the rest of the flock to us, hook, line, and sinker, which is our multitude.

Lift Your Rod

God has zero tolerance for pity parties when He has given us the Spiritual Tools to work with. Is this being a little insensitive? Absolutely not. When the enemy is on your track, trying to hold you back, do you think whimpering will help you? You must be prepared to use what God has already placed in your hands.

And if we do not know our reason for being by now, at this stage in the game, go back to the drawing board, reevaluate, redo, and reapproach. Why? The enemy is not playing with us or our Divine Destiny. His job is to prevent us from getting to our Predestined Blueprinted Promises, and if we sit on our hands, we will 'get got' by their antics. Here is what we need to know: *"And the LORD said to Moses, 'Why do you cry to Me? Tell the children of Israel to go forward. But lift up your rod, and stretch out your hand over the sea and divide it. And the children of Israel shall go on dry ground through the midst of the sea.'"* Exodus 14:15-16.

What if we are not Moses? Then my question would be, 'Do we not possess the same Spiritual Capacity as Moses?' We do! We cannot lay the blame elsewhere if we downplay our Divine Access. In all things, approach it *As It Pleases God*, taking ourselves out of the equation and putting His Divine Will at the forefront. What can this do for us? He will use us, doing what we could never do alone. Please allow me to Spiritually Align: *"But when they deliver you up, do not worry about how or what you should speak. For it will be given to you in that hour what you should speak; for it is not you who speak, but the Spirit of your Father who speaks in you."* Matthew 10:19-20.

Positively take the limits off yourself, your mind, and your thoughts while pumping the brakes on your emotions and negativity, and repeat this: *"Your word is a lamp to my feet and a light to my path."* Psalm 119:105. Everything will begin to work together for your good according to your Divine Purpose and Predestined Blueprint. Above all, if you find the GOOD or the WIN-WIN in all things, you can always find your way home as your inner compass guides you into GREATNESS. Many Blessings!

Dr. Y. Bur

www.ingramcontent.com/pod-product-compliance
Lightning Source LLC
Chambersburg PA
CBHW071437160426
43195CB00013B/1939